if stones could sing...
A Hindu American Story of Service and Devotion

if stones could sing... sing... sing...
this song of selfless service would ring.

- **Mahant Swami Maharaj**
  Inspirer of Akshardham

His Holiness Pramukh Swami Maharaj (1921–2016) was the visionary of Akshardham, North America.

શ્રી

અક્ષરધામમાં દરેકને જીવન ઘડતરની પ્રેરણા મળી અને જીવન દિવ્ય બને એવી ભગવાનને પ્રાર્થના.

શાસ્ત્રી નારાયણસ્વરૂપદાસ

In this Akshardham,
one and all will find inspiration to mold their life
and transcend spiritually.
For this, I offer my prayers to Bhagwan.

Shastri Narayanswarupdas
(Pramukh Swami Maharaj)

His Holiness Mahant Swami Maharaj, Pramukh Swami Maharaj's successor and the current guru, is the inspirer of Akshardham, North America.

Akshardham is Pramukh Swami Maharaj's spiritual and cultural gift to America. All are welcome.

There is no distinction between the murti that we see here and the one in Akshardham (God's abode).

Bhagwan Swaminarayan resides here along with his choicest devotee Gunatitanand Swami.

Through their divine presence our minds become still. And we experience peace and eternal bliss.

Bhagwan Swaminarayan will fulfill the prayers of all who visit and have his darshan here.

Akshardham is a reflection of the bhakti, seva, dedication and unity of thousands of bhaktas. It will inspire faith and kindness in the world.

Sadhu Keshavjivandas
Wednesday, 23rd August 2023
Akshardham, Robbinsville,
New Jersey. U.S.A

if stones could sing...
A Hindu American Story of Service and Devotion

Inspirer: HH Pramukh Swami Maharaj
Blessings: HH Mahant Swami Maharaj

1st Edition: September 2023

Copies: 25,000
Price: $3.00
ISBN: 978-1-947461-25-3

Copyright: © Swaminarayan Aksharpith
All rights reserved. No part of this book may be used or reproduced in any form or by any means without permission in writing from the publisher, except for brief quotations embodied in reviews and articles.

Published and Printed by
Swaminarayan Aksharpith
Shahibaug, Ahmedabad-4, India

Website: www.baps.org

CONTENTS

Foreword by Ishwarcharandas Swami — xv

Preface: One of Many Songs — xix

1. The Song of Stones:
   Embedded in Tradition, Embracing Innovation — 1

2. The Song of Bhakti:
   The Subtle Foundation of Akshardham — 31

3. The Song of Seva:
   The Steps to Akshardham — 45

4. The Song of Bhaktas:
   The Pillars of Akshardham — 59

5. The Song of Robbinsville, New Jersey:
   A Forever Home — 83

6. The Song of the Inspirers:
   Gurus as Exemplars of Bhakti and Seva — 99

7. Afterword: Your Song, Our Song — 113

Dedication

to the gurus,
who envision and inspire mandirs
within and without…

to the thousands of
skilled artisan volunteers, devotees, and sadhus,
who lived and served in harmony,
to construct this Hindu mandir,
the many before, and those yet to come.

The warmth and spiritual energy of the vast Akshardham campus invites visitors with abundant opportunity to clear the mind and experience the Divine.

Foreword

Over the last few months, I have stared out several times a day at the 189-foot-tall mahashikhar or central steeple of the Akshardham Mahamandir from the second-floor window of the sadhus' residence. It was as if each stone was speaking, singing, dancing. Each stone had a song to share—stories of selfless service, harmony, and devotion. I heard the stones calling out to Bhagwan Swaminarayan and the other Hindu deities to whom this mandir is dedicated. I heard the stones calling out to the sevaks and sadhus from around the world who helped complete it while putting their education, careers, and family matters on hold. I heard the stones singing to our gurus, Pramukh Swami Maharaj and Mahant Swami Maharaj, for inspiring its commencement and completion. Finally, I heard the stones calling out to the world—to the devoted and kind-hearted all over—Hindu or otherwise. Their song moved me. I realized it had the melody to move millions.

There is more than one story of BAPS Swaminarayan Akshardham in Robbinsville, New Jersey (Akshardham). Each volunteer or visitor hears a distinct song. But in sum, these stories knit together a musical of bhakti, seva, inclusiveness, commitment, Hindu integration, and American acceptance. The stories were so rich that I felt these first songs could inspire thousands more to be sung. I asked Yogi Trivedi to speak with the makers, sevaks, and the community members to hear their tunes. His unique background as a bhakta, research scholar, and lifelong student, who has written several publications on the Swaminarayan community, allows him to experience things often unheard by others. I asked him to share the stones' first songs. And to do so before Akshardham's public offering.

When the conceptual design of Akshardham first started, none of us knew that the result would be so majestic, so magnificent, so mammoth. The formation evolved with inspiration from both gurus, as well as from the bhakti and seva of the sadhus and volunteers who wanted to offer their love to God. The inspirer, Pramukh Swami Maharaj, said that the mandir was never meant to be a spectacle of power or strength but rather a symbol of devotion and dedication. This is why I strongly believe that the sacred pilgrimage centers of India can be experienced in this mandir in America. There is a sense of fulfillment and centeredness you will feel in the murtis' presence. Your prayers will be heard and fulfilled. I experience this regularly.

Though Akshardham stands as one of the most illustrious Hindu houses of worship in America, it is also a place for education and unity for all the cultural and religious communities of America. People from all walks of life have helped create and celebrate it. On behalf of our current guru, Mahant Swami Maharaj, and the satsang community, I invite all to visit.

On second thought, Akshardham is not ours to invite you to; it is yours to visit and experience. For Hindus and spiritual seekers, it is an oasis for prayer and serenity. For our neighbors and friends from other traditions, it is a means of interacting with the Hindu and Indian community. Finally, for students of culture and architecture, it is a center for learning. Come and experience it in person along with your loved ones.

Seeing is believing. Speak to the volunteers. Meditate beside the seekers. Observe the faces of visitors. Taste the traditional cuisine in the form of prasad. Admire the beauty of the intricate architecture. And listen closely to the stones singing. You may take their song of hope back to your community. It is a song that all of America and the world needs to hear and sing today.

Ishwarcharandas Swami
BAPS Swaminarayan Akshardham
Robbinsville, New Jersey, USA
13 August 2023

One of the first experiences of the Divine at the Akshardham complex is the 49-foot-tall murti of Bhagwan Swaminarayan's child-yogi form, Nilkanth Varni. Seen in yogic pose, the murti symbolizes the internal steadiness achieved from the spiritual journey. Visitors meditate, chant, and offer incense sticks in prayer to the murti.

Preface:
One of Many Songs

Growing up as a practicing Hindu on Long Island in New York, I valued acceptance and at times braved ridicule for being "the other." The difficulty was not that I identified as Hindu or that I physically looked Indian but that I was a religious Hindu who enjoyed Indian culture, cuisine, and spirituality, and often in public spaces. I distinctly remember the first time I wore my *tilak-chandlo* (sectarian mark of sandalwood and vermilion worn by Swaminarayan Hindus on the forehead) to school, when I presented on Hindu rituals and devotional music in high school, and when I listened to my peers speak about "idol worship," "red dots," and "cow and monkey gods". My peers were confused and at times shocked by the general portrayal of Hinduism. In hindsight, I do not think that they meant to be offensive or demeaning; it was that I simply did not have the tools and support to explain my faith's markers and expressions.

Hindus have come a long way in the last forty years in North America. There are thousands of cultural centers and *mandirs* (Hindu houses of worship) that serve more than 4.5 million Indian Americans. Professor Diana Eck's Pluralism Project at Harvard University documents the stories of many of them. The increase in the Hindu population and the general acceptance of Indian music and food in pop culture has been helpful. The external label from American society for Indian Americans as a "model minority," which is often attributed to the rise in education, professional station, financial independence, and low crime visibility, has also helped Indians earn a certain acceptance in society (though admittedly that term is not without fault). And yet, so much is left to be said.

Despite this growth in physical and material presence, many Hindus still have trouble articulating their own story in a way that is accessible to mainstream America. Who are Hindus? How do they worship? Why mandirs? What are their core beliefs? The list of questions continues. Part of the difficulty is also the vastness and diversity in Hinduism and Indian identity. Even though there are foundational similarities, no one story fits all. Without a clear narrative that speaks for (most of) the community, Hindus will struggle with being seen, heard, and understood by their neighbors, community leaders, and elected officials.

This short introduction to **BAPS Swaminarayan Akshardham, North America: A Landmark of Hindu Architecture and Culture**, is one of many modest, recent steps to address this need. The book not only shares the history of its making, but it flows through the guiding principles of Hinduism, which are the foundation for understanding the Hindu experience in the diaspora. Much more will be written in detail about the landmark's architecture, exhibits, and technology by experts. This book is not that. Think of this as a handbook distilling the experience at the BAPS Swaminarayan Akshardham complex in Robbinsville, New Jersey (Akshardham), and other Hindu mandirs in North America. Each chapter can be read independently, but as a book it weaves together the story of how Akshardham came to be through *bhakti* (devotion), *seva* (selfless service), inclusivity, the enthusiasm of the volunteers, and the inspiration from the gurus.

If one listens closely to the stones singing, one hears a tale of the spiritual growth of thousands. It is an account that is not easily told, and certainly not easily comprehended. I attempt it because Akshardham's public offering is bound to encourage the curious to inquire more.

Though it is a short read, and brevity is what readers prefer these days, this burdens the storyteller with the difficult task of omission. I spent many sleepless nights mulling over the limitations of space in this book. There are hundreds of other heroes whose tales are worthy of writing, but this minstrel can only share so many in 100 pages. I worry about who is left unmentioned. Alas, it is necessary to share a story, a song—to start somewhere. I try.

I did not think I was the right person for the task. But my mentor and guide, Pujya Ishwarcharandas Swami, reminded me that a certain distance and proximity are necessary when writing about people and places. Each affords its own benefits. Distance allows for clarity. Proximity allows for familiarity. I have been fortunate to have been blessed with both in the context of the Swaminarayan community, and specifically Akshardham. Though I was born into a Swaminarayan family and went on to study and research the community at Columbia University, I was not involved with the creation or the construction of Akshardham. I learned what community, service, equality, tradition, Hinduism, spirituality, and love meant in the Swaminarayan context in Robbinsville, New Jersey—almost 8,000 miles away from where the community was formed by Bhagwan Swaminarayan in the early nineteenth century—and I have many people to thank for this.

First and foremost, my guru, Mahant Swami Maharaj, blessed me several times while I was writing a draft, but then most visibly when the draft was complete. He penned the theme of the book, in which he insisted on emphasizing the word "sing" three times. We have published his words in his penmanship as the epigraph at the start of the book. He also wrote a special blessing for visitors and readers. I clearly remember that night. It was nearly 9:45 p.m., and he had met with hundreds of people earlier that evening. However, the guru's enthusiasm to serve set a benchmark for me. I am also humbled that Ishwarcharandas Swami wrote the Foreword. Not only does this lend the book his credible voice, but it also reminds me of how smoothly his thoughts and words flow on paper.

I am also grateful to several sadhus and volunteers for sharing information and experiences. One particular volunteer, who asked to remain unnamed, deserves special mention for sharing perspective critical to understanding the people and the past of this project. He was not alone. Many volunteers asked to have their names removed, for seva is done without desiring appreciation and recognition. For hundreds of people, Akshardham's story is important. Their own names and identities are not. I, too, wish that I was allowed to write *silently*.

One can only imagine how a draft written in twenty-five days may have first read. I would like to thank Bijal Jadav and Kshiti Vaghela for editing the final manuscript. I am grateful to Jaykishan Patel for giving my fleeting words visual form through his digital sketches and cover design. Krishnaswarupdas Swami's watercolor portraits of the gurus, Nilkanth Varni, and the Akshardham complex help the reader visualize my descriptions. I am thankful to Yogvivekdas Swami, who is always a comforting yet pointed first reader. Finally, I am grateful to Shantmurtidas Swami and the *sadhus* (monks) at BAPS Shri Swaminarayan Mandir, Atlanta, for a warm writing sanctuary; and to Anandananddas Swami, who let me use his workspace with a view to edit the manuscript.

The book includes words from several languages. I prefer to use Indic words over their English translations, especially when it refers to a key concept or belief. The Sanskrit or Gujarati word appears italicized the first time it appears in the text, along with a brief definition in parentheses. Though it seems to burden the text, it carries the benefit of familiarizing the reader with the tradition and its many languages.

Hinduism is a sensory religion—the often-overwhelming but crucial sights, sounds, scents, and textures must be consumed continuously. This book will answer only enough of your questions to convince you to visit. Perhaps then on your second visit, you will come looking for the interactions mentioned in the book with the Divine, the volunteers, and the architecture. It is only one of many songs. As an awe-inspiring symbol for Hindu faith, culture, and architecture, Akshardham serves as a place for all to belong, celebrate, and selflessly articulate pride for their tradition while integrating open-mindedly within the America that we love and now call home. It will serve as a bridge between many countries, religions, and cultures for generations to come.

Yogi Trivedi
5 August 2023

The final stone (*amalak*) is placed on the main steeple of the
Akshardham Mahamandir (16 June 2023),
marking the structural completion of the traditional stone mandir.
The stones sail more than 21,500 miles before finally resting at Akshardham.

1

The Song of Stones: Embedded in Tradition, Embracing Innovation

UNDERSTANDING AKSHARDHAM

She is patient, warm, and at once lively. The tour guide volunteer gives an easy, lucid explanation of every ritual visitors encounter on the Akshardham campus. Each word resonates with the passion and practicality she tries to live as a *bhakta* (believer). And then a curveball surprises her. For the visitor, it is probably the simplest, most elementary question he could ask. For the tour guide, it is a question that sends her into a series of stutters. He asks, "What is Akshardham?" She is not alone. Many people struggle to answer this question, not because they do not know, but because they have "too much" to share. As a landmark for Hindu faith, culture, and architecture, Akshardham aims to contribute so vastly to the community that it is difficult to explain concisely.

Akshardham has several components. Though many people only visualize the large, soft white mandir with its red and white flags waving at the top of the steeples, when they hear 'Akshardham', the entire campus is referred to as BAPS Swaminarayan Akshardham or simply Akshardham. The Akshardham Mahamandir (Mahamandir) is the heart of that campus. It is surrounded by a garland-like path, or *parikrama*, which functions as an ornate covered walkway to the Mahamandir. The campus also has a Welcome Center, smaller ritual mandir made of marble, a learning center, and more. Before we walk through the campus, it is important to understand why Akshardham is the center of creation for the community.

What is Akshardham? **Akshardham is a mandir and a cultural center. At its core, Akshardham is a home for, or an abode, of the Divine, where millions will come to experience spiritual tranquility and cultural celebrations. It is a living experience of spirituality and humanity. Akshardham is a product of bhakti and seva in a visual, permanent form. Akshardham is also a hub for bhakti and seva to amplify their impact on society.**

People often wonder why so much is put into the building of mandirs. The reason is that Indian temple architecture is a visual expression of faith. Akshardham is a grand and at once nuanced representation of Hindu faith, history, and lifestyle. Visual elements are a highly effective way to transmit these elements to subsequent generations. When spoken words could not be recorded and written manuscripts were brittle, these mandirs carried forth the story of a time and people to future generations. Stories from sacred and historical texts, great saints and seers, mystical poets, and philosophers all find a place to sing in the mandir's architecture. They share something about the time in which they were built and the communities who built them. Each mandir carries the distinct cultural stamp of a people for future generations to remember and celebrate.

Akshardham takes on a slightly unique and significant theological importance than other mandirs in the Swaminarayan tradition. The term "Akshardham" literally means the divine residence of Bhagwan Swaminarayan. The *dham* (abode) named *Akshar* or *Aksharbrahma* (a metaphysical entity that leads one to the Divine; the God-realized guru) is where Bhagwan Swaminarayan resides in his glory and divinity. It is where every spiritual aspirant aims to rest upon achieving *moksha* (spiritual release) and transcendence. That same *Aksharbrahma* manifests on Earth in human form as the God-realized guru. This Akshardham then is a physical representation of where Bhagwan Swaminarayan resides in his divine abode, and thus where one comes to experience the Divine on Earth. This may be the reason why so many visitors experience a sense of serenity and spiritual stimulation upon entering the campus. After all, it is God's residence.

EMBEDDED IN TRADITION: AKSHARDHAM IN THE CONTEXT OF SACRED ARCHITECTURE

The design of Akshardham brings together functionality, the age-old tradition of temple construction, and technological innovation. Religious architecture was codified extensively over the last 1,600 years in India and Asia. In addition to being houses of worship and centers for cultural and social interaction, mandirs are a key medium for preservation and transmission. Stone mandirs were symbols of authority, pride, and identity. They were often at the center of a city. Expectedly, these mandirs were among the first objects of attack by rivals or foreign forces and were unfortunately desecrated in the thousands amid such strife. They were also built in large quantities. Mandirs in Asia evolved over time in design and concept based on utility and patronage from rulers and religious communities. For example, one sees the presence of colonial British guards in a mandir in old Delhi and Jain merchants in mandirs in Ahmedabad's inner old city.

Architecture is an expression of the sacred in India. These expressions are highly sophisticated disciplines. The ancient Hindu sacred texts are intentionally particular about how mandirs must be constructed. This is why mandir architecture is thought of as a *shastra* (sacred science or faculty). Over time, temple-building is theorized and studied from sacred texts known as the *Shilpa-shastras* and *Vastu-shastras* (sacred carving and architectural treatises). Each of the mandir architectural styles is documented in various texts in different regions and centuries. Some of the more prominent texts include the *Vishnu Dharmaottar Purana* (7th century), *Agni Purana* (9th century), *Shilpa Prakash* (9th century), *Mayamattam* (11th century), *Samrangan Sutradhar* (11th century), and *Aparajitpraccha* (12th century). Most of these texts are written in Sanskrit. Some later texts include drawings, and all texts include detailed instructions about the types of materials to use, measurements and proportions, shape of designs, sacred building techniques, and the directions that the mandir *murtis* (sacred image of the Divine) must face. Sacred architecture remains quite an elaborate technical and scriptural affair today for Hindus, as well as Buddhists and Jains.

Two key mandir *shailis* (methods or styles of construction) became prominent over time. The Nagara style is popular in northern and western India. The Dravidian style is popular in southern India. Regional variants in eastern and central India evolved as well. Each sub-tradition also developed its own style of architecture based on their ritual and functional needs. Larger mandirs became rare after the eighteenth century. In Gujarat, Bhagwan Swaminarayan and certain Jain community leaders revived the tradition of building large stone mandirs. Bhagwan Swaminarayan built six mandirs during his manifested lifetime (1781–1830). His community continued to build hundreds in the first two hundred years after his passing. Pramukh Swami Maharaj (1921–2016), the fifth spiritual successor to Bhagwan Swaminarayan, further revived the tradition of stone architecture mandirs by building the Akshardham complexes in Gandhinagar and New Delhi, India, and other traditional stone mandirs in the United Kingdom, Canada, and USA. These temples became a source of pride and identity for Hindus and Indians around the world. This mandir-building renaissance also encouraged other Hindu communities to build their own expressions of faith. Today the entire Swaminarayan Hindu community has over 4,000 mandirs around the world. More than 1,200 of those mandirs have been built by Pramukh Swami Maharaj and BAPS Swaminarayan Sanstha.

A cohort of Indian architects, structural engineers, and scholars recently visited Akshardham in Robbinsville. The guide could hear them whispering as they gasped at the spires, external walls, and interior ceilings of the Mahamandir. What started off as a debate ended in an intense exchange between two experts. They could not agree on the predominant architectural style, regional influence, and time period emulated in the architecture. The guide intervened and promised to introduce them to senior sadhus and designers who would address their queries. Upon closer look, the group concluded this was a Nagara style mandir. Their debate was well founded. The reason that it was difficult to discern the temple building tradition of Akshardham is because of how the architecture is embedded in the tradition of western India, while innovating with influences from other parts of India and the world. Pramukh Swami Maharaj preferred building mandirs in the Nagara tradition, while also encouraging the sadhus and designers to innovate with technology and creative designs. But he also insisted they balance that innovation by following the guidelines of the past. He urged the sadhus to learn from other mandirs and research Sanskrit scriptures and treatises to revive the age-old Hindu tradition of temple architecture. This is not to say that the

Mahamandir imitates any particular structure's design. Rather, it resonates with an organic development of design, one that is rooted in tradition but also embraces novelty and addresses functionality in the American and New Jersey context.

AKSHARDHAM: MILESTONES AND TIMELINE

The history of Akshardham dates back to when the first immigrants left India in the last century. The Gujarati diaspora grew through trade and labor opportunities, first in East Africa and then in the United Kingdom from the 1900s onward. Immigration to America significantly opened to Indians in search of education and career opportunities in the 1960s. They, too, brought with them their culture, religion, and rituals.

Hindu mandir construction in America saw an uptick in the 1970s. BAPS Shri Swaminarayan Mandir in Queens, New York, was one of the first in the region. The mandir held weekly assemblies and provided support to those from several Indic religious communities looking for a cultural, religious, and social home away from home. The community's presence grew and so did the presence of BAPS mandirs across the country. Mandirs in Atlanta, Chicago, Houston, and Los Angeles flourished with the growth of the Hindu community. These early mandirs were built in existing community centers or were constructed in contemporary style. Pramukh Swami Maharaj traveled from coast to coast via car to meet the spiritual and cultural needs of Indians settling in the country. The guru toiled for days on end during the 1970s and 1980s, sowing the seeds for a united and devoted Hindu community across the nation. The result of these efforts became more apparent years later when mandirs began to spring up in small towns and secondary cities across America.

The Hindu and Indian population in New Jersey meanwhile was growing beyond imagination. Pramukh Swami Maharaj inspired the first BAPS Swaminarayan Mandir in New Jersey in the town of Edison in 1991, as a culmination of the Cultural Festival of India celebrated just a few miles away. For the first time in America, this festival raised awareness about the various regional traditions of Indian art, music, food, and customs on a grand scale. The success of this festival set the tone for Indian cultural ambassadorship in America. In the coming years, New Jersey would become home to some seven BAPS mandirs. As the community grew across the nation, the guru blessed the building of traditional stone mandirs as centers of cultural pride, spiritual awareness, and devotion. He also inspired the building of Akshardham in New Jersey as the last project so the nation's Hindus could take part and contribute to its development. In 2004, traditional stone mandirs were inaugurated in Houston and Chicago. In 2007, similar mandirs were inaugurated in Toronto and Atlanta. In 2012, a mandir was built in Chino Hills (outside of Los Angeles). Then came the time for the pinnacle of these architectural masterpieces to be commenced—Akshardham in New Jersey.

In 1984 while in Hackettstown, New Jersey, Pramukh Swami Maharaj shared his desire to build mandirs in America that would draw people from all over the world. In 1997, he called local leaders of the community and expressed his wish to build Akshardham in New Jersey. Local leaders started the long and arduous search for suitable land shortly thereafter. Pramukh Swami Maharaj also visited several of the potential sites in 1998, 2000, and 2004. After a Central Jersey town rejected the plans for a Hindu mandir in their community, BAPS found this parcel of land in Robbinsville Township. In 2008, the land was procured by the devotees. Work for the marble mandir and the cultural center began in 2010. Pramukh Swami Maharaj traveled to New Jersey for fourteen days in 2014 at the age of 92. He inaugurated the mandir, performed the *murti-pratishtha* (Hindu ritual for consecrating a murti through which the guru infuses the spirit of the Divine into the murtis) and broke ground for the construction of the Mahamandir. Construction of the Mahamandir commenced in 2015.

There are several milestones in the construction process in sacred Hindu construction. Per the ancient architectural treatises, there are certain rituals that must be performed before commencing various construction phases. More than two dozen such rituals were performed drawing in blessings, appreciating the artisan volunteers, and marking the commencement of key components, such as the foundation, *mandovar* (main outer wall), *shikhars* (tall steeples), *samarans* (shorter, trapezoidal spires; also known as *phamsana shikhars*), and the placement of the final stone on the *mahashikhar* (central steeple). The inauguration of the Mahamandir was marked with the start of the Festival of Inspirations on 25 June 2023. The festival concludes with the murti-pratishtha and public offering of the Mahamandir in the Fall of 2023.

STONES SAILING THE SEAS

The stones sing at Akshardham because they have witnessed and weathered beyond all others. Imagine traveling alongside a stone quarried in Bulgaria, Turkey, Greece, or Italy. What would the trek of almost 21,500 miles entail before settling in Robbinsville? This is the story of their journey.

Several different types of stones were used in the construction of Akshardham. The ritual, or *shikharbaddha* (traditionally constructed steepled), mandir is made of Italian marble, and therefore unable to withstand the cold northeastern winters. The mandir is hence encased in a modern structure to preserve the stone and carvings. The Mahamandir, in contrast, stands in the open. The designers required a stone that could tolerate the region's weather patterns. They searched in India and Europe. A stone expert suggested that they find a stone that had already proven it could last the test of time in a similar climate since Indian limestone was not suitable for this environment. Consultants directed the sadhus and community leaders to limestone mines in Bulgaria. The stone had initially been considered during the construction of the BAPS Swaminarayan Mandir in London way back in

1991. The mandir architects and designers toured the capital city of Sofia and noticed that the architectural masterpieces of the city had all been made using Bulgarian limestone. Samples were taken from several different quarries and sent to America for lab testing for durability, structural strength, and climate compatibility. After six months, the testing confirmed that the Bulgarian limestone would be ideal for the exterior of the edifice. In addition, several Indian sandstones, namely Bijolia, Bansi Paharpur, Jodhpur, and Balesar, are used for the walls and beams on the ground floor. South Indian granite is also used for some structural work. The interior of the Mahamandir is built with a milky, smooth marble from Thasos, Greece. Some of the statuettes of the celestial beings and bhaktas specifically in the *Paramhansa Mandapam* (hall with inverted, ornate ceilings dedicated to the principal disciples of Bhagwan Swaminarayan) are made from a special, stark white Italian marble which allows for precise carving. Close to two million cubic feet of these various types of stone were quarried, shipped, and carved for the Akshardham Mahamandir in Robbinsville, New Jersey. **BAPS has planted more than 2 million trees worldwide to offset the impact of stone construction on the environment.**

All these stones were quarried in a record amount of time, checked for defects, and packed and shipped to the Port of Mundra in Kutch, Gujarat, India. The stones went through a customs and clearance process before being loaded onto trucks and shipped to one of several sites in and around Pindwada, Rajasthan. Dozens of trucks transported containers of stone over this 250-mile journey. In Rajasthan, the stones were checked again for damage. Damaged stone would result in structural weakness and aesthetic defects, but also disregard scriptural mandate.

The Sompura architects (traditional architects) cut the stones according to the sizes allocated for each part of the Mahamandir. These stones were then passed on to the skilled artisans who shaped them. These stones were then hand carved by specialists to replicate the traditional designs. Skilled artisans worked at sites in Rajasthan to shape, carve, and polish the stone. The artisans found stable work for close to a decade and were able to stay close to home.

For the first time in the history of Indian temple building, a mandir of this scale was dry fitted in Rajasthan before being shipped to the United States. Dry fitting is an innovative concept in which all the stones or replicas are assembled true to size on site in India, before being coded, dismantled, and shipped. The mandirs are assembled like a large jigsaw puzzle. There are two advantages to this method. First, it enables flexibility for the designers and traditional architects to fix minor flaws in measurements that could affect the fitting. A few millimeters off in design or stone cutting could potentially lead to significant delays during assembly. Second, this helps the architects to better appreciate the true scale and size of the Mahamandir before shipping. This then allows the sadhus and volunteers to adapt designs of components in real time. For example, when the mandovar and the *stambha* (pillars) of the Mahamandir were dry fitted, the designers were able to make changes that complemented the motif, scale, and layout. This dry fitting permitted the designers to keep the design fluid as they saw the mandir come to life.

Once the sections of the Mahamandir were inspected and dry fitted, they were disassembled and passed on to the skilled artisans to fine tune the carving and slightly polish. The stones would need to be further carved and polished to perfection in New Jersey. It is important to note that assembling and disassembling the stone pieces required a unique skill. These skills would be needed again once the stones were unpacked, organized, and reassembled in New Jersey. Now the carved stones were ready to leave India. They were packed, transported, and fumigated in trucks to the Port of Mundra, from where they began a more than 8,000-mile journey to the Port of New Jersey in Newark and Elizabeth. In New Jersey, they would find a home for the next thousand years.

STONES SETTLING IN NEW JERSEY

The first stones for the Mahamandir arrived in the Summer of 2014. Once the stones arrive at the port, there is a detailed clearing and safety process. The containers are then transported by road to Robbinsville, New Jersey. The stones were removed from the crates and stacked in an open space according to a sophisticated coding system. This was the key to assembling the mandir efficiently.

There is a specific way to open these boxes so that the

carved stones within are not damaged. The skilled artisan volunteers from India knew exactly how to open these boxes to prevent mishap. They taught local volunteers the process. The stones were then taken to an adjacent lot where they were cleaned, dried, and doused in a special composition to increase their durability.

Another team of volunteers would then chip away at the rear of the stones where the grouting material is applied. For the adhesive to hold the stones in place, the stones need a rough, chipped surface. This helps the stones lock into place with adjacent stones. Creating these *"tantcha"* (rough surfaces) is a trademark sight and sound of a stone architectural construction site. It catches the attention of visitors who come for *darshan* (viewing or beholding of a sacred image of the deity with reverence) at the ritual mandir in Robbinsville. It is also symbolic of the volunteer molding his own self through service. Women volunteers from around the country also trained under these skilled artisan volunteers and made considerable contributions. The volunteers believed that the sincerity and dedication they put into sculpting and chipping away at the stone would in turn shape their own character and persona. **Building Akshardham is a way to build oneself.**

Once it is a stone's turn to settle into its new home, it is transported by lull and often lifted by crane to its resting place in the Mahamandir. After being assembled, the stones are again polished, cleaned, treated with waterproof agents, and fixed if the carvings were damaged or overly polished. The process seems straightforward, but the stones also sing of the difficulties in the building process.

Building an architectural marvel of this magnitude far away from India also naturally had issues of cultural translation, timing, transport of material, and volunteers. It was difficult to explain and show the traditional stone building process to local town inspectors and state governing agencies. Many did not believe that the mandir could stand and support its own weight in this manner. Second, transporting the stones and the materials needed to work with this stone was not easy or always cost-effective. An entire factory-type set up was needed to unload, treat, refine, and assemble the stones. Finally, it was difficult to find skilled artisan volunteers to help build the mandir, and even more complex to find a team of supporting volunteers who could work under their supervision and guidance. And yet, the Mahamandir was completed in approximately seven-and-a-half years and with the guidance of local officials.

This was only possible because people from all walks of life came together to give life to the stones. The stories of integration and service continue to astonish those who hear them. Many such stories will be shared in the following chapters. BAPS' novel and complex system of integration of full-time volunteers from all over the world in the creation of this Mahamandir only adds to its marvel.

The making of the Mahamandir in Robbinsville is not the story of just local or regional volunteers, but one of an entire community. Many of these volunteers had served for short durations over the past few years, but this effort was different. Hundreds of volunteers chose to put their education or professional and social lives on hold and relocate to Robbinsville to help finish building the Mahamandir. Whether on a short-term basis for a few days or weeks or a longer-term basis for six to eighteen months or a full-time basis for several years, thousands of volunteers from around North America selflessly gave their time to the construction of the Mahamandir, working under the direction and guidance of and side-by-side with skilled artisan volunteers from India.

For some of these volunteers, who had never worked on a traditional stone temple construction project before, there was a fifteen-day certificate orientation program set up for the long-term volunteers which included both theoretical and practical lessons on temple architecture and its construction process. These long-term volunteers were in turn able to share this knowledge with short-term volunteers from all over North America.

More than fifty young sadhus and sadhus-in training who had experience building temples in India came to join the efforts. These young sadhus shared their knowledge and experience of temple construction with the volunteers and worked alongside the skilled artisan volunteers. Thousands from all over the world donated their time to serve in the construction of the mandir. Some of these volunteers took on the task of feeding, serving, and helping with the logistics of the construction volunteers as well.

Volunteers from the community took the initiative to certify as safety instructors and inspectors. They led special safety seminars and inspected the site to intervene and stop any processes that could lead to a safety-related event. They worked with independent consultants to raise the standard of safety and to protect the volunteers. Safety became the benchmark for success among the volunteers.

The role of women volunteers in such stonework in the building of the mandir is also pioneering. Women volunteered to waterproof the stones, operate lulls, assemble and build stone structures under the supervision of the skilled volunteers, and even led their own teams to rebar concrete. Their passion and dedication moved all those who witnessed them serve day in and day out. Never before have women volunteers so heavily engaged in the process of building a Hindu mandir. When asked what she thought of her role in building the Mahamandir, a young IT professional said, "It is *my* mandir. I can say it with a sense of ownership. This mandir is not just built for me. It was built by me. What I have learned in the process will mold me and change me for the rest of my life. I will bring my children here from Ohio and tell them that their mother answered her guru's call to serve and helped complete this mandir."

AKSHARDHAM: THE COMPLEX AND ITS COMPONENTS

The Mahamandir, looking over the rest of the complex, is certainly the central component. However, there are several other components that are imperative to the complete spiritual, cultural, and architectural experience. Here is what you may encounter on your visit.

Upon driving into the campus, visitors are first met by the 49-foot, golden-hued, bronze murti of Nilkanth Varni, or the child-yogi form of Bhagwan Swaminarayan, who left his home at the age of eleven and traveled across the Indian subcontinent. Standing tall in a one-legged, austere, yogic posture, with his eyes closed and mind reflecting inward, Nilkanth Varni reminds visitors of the balance between the courage required to achieve in life while remaining grounded within and submitting to the Divine. The murti's height celebrates the forty-nine years Bhagwan Swaminarayan lived. Upon entering the **Nilkanth Vatika (Nilkanth Plaza)**, visitors will find a map that explains his journey through India. There are also seven valuable lessons from his journey for the spiritual aspirant to read and reflect on in his presence. Pilgrims are welcome to meditate, chant mantras, and offer incense sticks as common Indic forms of prayer and worship.

Just past the path to Nilkanth Varni is the **Brahma Kund**. The Brahma Kund is a large body of water modeled after the iconic stepwells of western India. Mandirs were the center of social interaction in ancient towns and cities. The devout often traveled for several hours or even days to visit these pilgrimage sites. Before entering the mandir, there would be a place for them to rid the thoughts, worries, and burdens of routine life while preparing oneself to take in the aura of the Divine. The

Brahma Kund symbolizes the formal entry into Akshardham, where one can purify one's mind and thoughts—clear one's psychological and emotional headspace—before interacting with the Divine. The intricate stone-carved beauty of the step-pond pays homage to the great stepwells of Gujarat, namely Rani ki Vav in Patan and the Adalaj Stepwell outside of Amdavad, which are celebrations of architecture and civilization in western India. The water in the Brahma Kund represents the four sacred rivers of India, namely Ganga, Yamuna, Sarasvati, and Sarayu. One can find murtis representing the river goddesses along with details about the rivers' contributions to Indian civilization. The step-pond also includes waters from various other sacred bodies of water in India.

Visitors are greeted at the **Welcome Center**, where they can plan their visit with the help of guide-volunteers and watch an introductory video about the community and the campus. The foyer of the Welcome Center is an architectural marvel carved of teakwood. The style of architecture is prominently seen in *havelis* (traditional wooden homes) in Gujarat, India. Within the intricately carved wood enclosures, one notices close to four thousand *diyas* (sacred lamps). These lamps represent the joy and purity of life. Diwali, or the Hindu festival of lights, is celebrated with diyas. A walk through the traditional foyer reminds visitors to embrace a grateful mindset for the joy of each day.

After passing through the Welcome Center, visitors meet with a grand revealing—a eureka moment. It is the first point from where one has an unobstructed view of the Mahamandir. One gazes at the Mahamandir from a distance, right before entering the courtyard which has two reflection ponds and is surrounded by a **stone parikrama** (covered walkway surrounding the Mahamandir). The parikrama represents a circular garland around the abode of the Divine. Pilgrims perform *pradakshina* (circumambulation) as a sign of placing the Divine at the center of their world. The parikrama provides a path sheltered from rain, snow, and heat to perform the ritual around the Mahamandir.

Across the Welcome Center, devotees who are coming to the mandir for prayer and daily rituals with the community enter the ritual, marble shikharbaddha mandir. These mandirs have specific daily rituals performed by the priestly sadhus and devotees. The mandir is not "small," just smaller than the Mahamandir. Inside the mandir, one will experience a variety of rituals being performed several times a day, including *arti* (waving of lighted wicks before deities), *thal/bhog* (offering food to the deities), and *bhajan/kirtan* (singing devotional song). The schedule of the deities is quite structured and therefore darshan is only available at certain times. Though there are worship rituals at the Mahamandir, they only occur twice a day and darshan is still possible for visitors and pilgrims throughout the day. If one has the time, a visit to the shikharbaddha mandir is recommended to better experience Hindu ritual and daily worship. The architecture is also one of a kind. It is the first Hindu marble mandir in an encased structure.

AKSHARDHAM: THE MAHAMANDIR

The **Akshardham Mahamandir** is the very soul of the Akshardham complex. Devotees in the BAPS Swaminarayan tradition experience it as the heart and dwelling of the Divine—a form of Aksharbrahma. The Mahamandir has several different components. One first notices the large stone stairway leading up to the main entrance of the mandir. Climbing these steps is part of the ritual exercise of entering the mandir. It humbles the aspirant and allows him or her to persevere to reach the Divine.

The *jagati* (base plinth) of the mandir is referred to as the **Wisdom Plinth**. The entire Mahamandir, both structurally and thematically, rests on this base plinth. This plinth narrates profound messages about everyday wisdom from the Vachanamrut, Vedas, Ramayana, Mahabharata, and Shrimad Bhagavad Gita. The jagati also pays homage to the great poets, bhaktas, philosophers, sages and seers, as well as community leaders of India and the Western World. Here, one can find statuettes of inspirational figures from all communities and ethnic backgrounds. There are representations of female poets and bhaktas as well. The Sikh gurus, Mahavirji, Buddha, and several devotees and pioneers from faith-based communities are also celebrated. Several Dalit (Scheduled Class) devotees from marginalized sections of society are also celebrated here. Do not be surprised to find Classics thinkers, such as Socrates, and American leaders, such as President Abraham Lincoln and Dr. Martin Luther King, Jr., sharing wisdom here. The jagati has thirteen layers. The first layer is made of granite followed by twelve more layers of limestone to strengthen the wall.

On top of the base plinth is the **mandovar** (main outer wall) of the Mahamandir. The mandovar pays homage to great poets, bhaktas, philosophers, sages, and seers. An entire section of the mandovar is dedicated to Indian classical dance and music. Dancing postures of the ancient dance form called Bharatanatyam are carved as a tribute to Bhagwan Shiva. Scholars conducted months of research to find a complete listing of the 108 dancing postures seen here, and even greater research went into the depiction of the musical instruments from ancient times. Some of these instruments are now not known or played in India today, but they are depicted based on various *Sangit-shastra* texts (ancient treatises on music). The Chidambaram Nataraja Mandir (10th century) in Tamil Nadu, India, also depicts Bhagwan Shiva's 108 dancing postures. However, the tribute to Bhagwan Shiva and Indian classical dance and music in modern times, and that too in the West, makes the depictions here at the Mahamandir unique. One also notices an ode to elephants, who carried heavy stones and timber in the building of mandirs for centuries. They are often included on the walls of mandirs to express gratitude for their services in the traditional building process. Visitors can walk around the exterior of the jagati and mandovar to admire the architecture and learn from its messages.

Above the walls and ceiling, there are nine large shikhars (towered steeples) and nine samarans (shorter, trapezoidal steeples; also known as *phamsana shikhar*). Each of these steeples or spires covers different shrines and ceilings within the Mahamandir. At the center of it all, visitors will notice the mahashikhar (central steeple). The mahashikhar's size is impressive, standing 189-foot-tall and connecting the entire area of the **Paramhansa Mahamandapam** (the central large, pillared hall dedicated to Bhagwan Swaminarayan's disciples) beneath it. The mahamandapam is approximately 80 feet in length and width. A mahashikhar and mahamandapam of this scale are rare to find in modern mandir construction.

One then approaches the entrance of the Mahamandir, first encountering the **Pravesh Choki** (entrance porch) and the **Swagat Mandapam** (vestibule). This porch houses unique designs and representations of nature and the Divine. It also has depictions of various Hindu sites of pilgrimage. The visitor then enters the first and most important hall of the Mahamandir known as the **Parabrahma Mandapam**. This hall is dedicated to Bhagwan Swaminarayan. It depicts incidents from his life through various murtis of his manifested form. It is from this mandir that one's eyes first settle on the **Mukhya Garbhagruh** (central shrine), which is located straight ahead at the center of the Mahamandir.

After darshan in the central shrine, one arrives at the largest hall of the Mahamandir. The **Paramhansa Mandapam** or the **mahamandapam** is the largest pillared hall in any existing mandir in the world to date. The intentional placement of the pillars accommodates enough space for devotees and visitors to gather and have darshan of the sacred images in the **Mukhya Garbhagruh**. Mandirs generally have many pillars to support the weight of the stones and spires. Here, the innovation allows for the pillars to be spread at the periphery. This mandapam has 7-foot-tall statuettes of Bhagwan Swaminarayan's foremost sadhus, who were known as *paramhansas* (sadhus with swan-like pure spirituality). The 78 statuettes, carved from a stark white Italian marble, can be seen with musical instruments, sacred texts, and other tools of service prescribed to each one in the community's sacred texts. Many of these senior sadhus were poets, musicians, theologians, and social reformers, who changed the landscape of western India and modern Hinduism. Statuettes of this size and precision have never before been carved and installed in a mandir.

There are three other notable domed halls. The **Aksharbrahma Mandapam** celebrates the life of Bhagwan Swaminarayan's first successor. Gunatitanand Swami is regarded as a God-realized guru who embodied the Divine within himself. He is also thought of as Bhagwan Swaminarayan's abode—Akshardham. The current guru is the manifestation of Aksharbrahma. Thus, this hall is dedicated to the metaphysical form of Akshardham. The **Aishwarya Mandapam** celebrates the various manifestations of the Divine and gurus in Indic traditions, such as Surdas, Tukaram, Narsinh Mehta, and others. There are 160 statuettes in this mandapam. The **Mukta Mandapam** celebrates the devotees par excellence of the Swaminarayan tradition, who serve as role models for those who wish to excel on the spiritual path. There are 90 statuettes in this hall. There are other large mandapams (halls) with inverted domes inside the Mahamandir. The messaging and carving in the halls and the pillars that support them are one of a kind. Most importantly, all the inverted ceilings are distinctive.

Once one's eyes settle from the overwhelming architecture, the bhakta finally views the Divine. The heart of the Mahamandir is its 12 *garbha gruhas* (shrines) and 1 *mahagarbhagruha* (central shrine). In Hinduism, the one Divine manifests in different forms. The shrines house the murtis of various manifestations of the Divine from around India. Murtis of Shri Lakshmi Narayan Bhagwan, Shri Tirupati Balaji-Padmavati Bhagwan, Shri Parvati-Shankar Bhagwan, Shri Sita-Ram Bhagwan, Shri Radha-Krishna Bhagwan, Shri Rukmini and Vithoba, Shri Ganesh ji and Shri Kartikeya ji, and Shri Hanuman ji and Shri Lakshman ji are installed in these shrines. The central shrine houses the murti of Bhagwan Swaminarayan with Gunatitanand Swami (Akshar-Purushottam Maharaj). The Mahamandir is inclusive in its theological nature so that worshippers from all traditions and geographic regions will find solace in the form of the Divine they worship. It aims to make Hindus of various Indian regions and sub-traditions from all over America feel at home while they worship.

The Mahamandir has two floors. The first floor (located below the floor housing the shrines) includes the **Abhishek Mandapam**, where the faithful can engage in the ritual bathing of the Divine to pray for the completion of a noble task or simply for inner peace and stability. The abhishek ritual is a popular ritual in Hindu mandirs often only performed by priests and sadhus. Here, everyone can engage in the ritual after washing their hands and purifying their minds.

AKSHARDHAM: BEFORE YOU LEAVE

In addition to the Mahamandir, there will be a **Museum and Learning Center** depicting the making of Akshardham and an introduction to Indian civilization, Hinduism, and the Swaminarayan tradition. This three-floor museum is slated to open in 2024. Finally, the courtyard will also feature a musical fountain show based on a core lesson of humanity and integrity found in the ancient Hindu scriptures. Visitors can also visit the **Akshardham Gift Store** to take home souvenirs and publications. The international culinary treats at **Shayona Cafe** are celebrated by local tour guides and food critics. And it is all sanctified and offered to the Divine by the bhaktas before making it available to visitors.

This is the Akshardham experience in short. **More than 10,000 statues and statuettes of various sizes, including 2,400 stone tablet murals, depict the lessons of the past and present for the future, utilizing approximately 2 million cubic feet of stone in the creation of the Mahamandir and stone parikrama.** The detail and nuance are unlike any carved mandir. In some instances, the carvings are almost half a foot deep! The words on these pages do not do justice to the beauty of the Mahamandir nor do they completely capture the depth of the stones and their songs. For this, one must visit and take it in with all senses. Akshardham, like much of Hinduism, is a sensory, in-person experience.

EMBRACING INNOVATION: ORIGINALITY WITHIN TRADITION

It is no surprise that the Mahamandir opened in 2023 uses some of the best technology to support devotion and ritual. Advanced lighting aids in the darshan of the sacred images and detailed study of the carvings. The heated floor within the Mahamandir and along the mandovar allows for visitors to explore the outside in the fall and winter seasons. The green technology utilized for power consumption and the foundation considers the health of our planet. The list of technological advancements is extensive, but innovation at Akshardham does not end there.

Symbolism is everything in temple architecture. The originality in the messaging used throughout the Mahamandir truly stands apart. Flora and fauna have long been celebrated within temple construction. Lotuses are celebrated for being pure even while growing within bodies of water and mud. Peacocks are seen as celestial birds that represent regality, patience, and compassion. They are also associated with Saraswati ji (the goddess of wisdom). Several such contributors to our ecosystem are cherished in the Mahamandir architecture with never before used designs and detail.

Foundational aspects articulated through stone murals with such detail and intention is also an innovation at Akshardham. Many of the messages of ancient Hindu wisdom are made accessible to the modern visitor in America. The Mahamandir also emphasizes the importance of preserving literature, art, music, and dance. The carvings of musical instruments, classical dance postures, and the mystical poets of India have never been so exhaustive in a Hindu mandir. The Mahamandir emphasizes that there is no discrimination based on caste, creed, color, gender, or status in God's eyes. In line with the Vedic verse that asks for the free flow of "good thoughts from all directions", the Mahamandir includes poets, thinkers, bhaktas, and community leaders from all backgrounds and parts of the world. The summation of all these parts, and their physical, mental, and emotional elements, supports the Mahamandir as a center for spiritual unity and integration.

BEYOND THE STONES

Akshardham's stones sing striking tunes of volunteerism, unity, and perseverance in the context of modern temple construction. The circumstances around the building of Akshardham were unique given the external challenges, scale and intricacy, as well as the project's global supply chain. The long-term coming together of skilled artisan volunteers, sadhus, and men and women bhaktas who donated their time, skills, and resources to the completion of this Mahamandir comprises its strong foundation and is the most mellifluous of songs sung by these stones.

The story of stones is the first, most apparent song the visitor hears. It is of Akshardham's physical and conceptual presence. However, there are other, more subtle songs that are equally compelling. These songs help one understand why, for whom, by who, through whose inspiration, and in which community Akshardham was built. The rest of this book is dedicated to this subtle foundation of Akshardham—songs of bhakti, seva, bhaktas, the inspiring gurus, and the Robbinsville community which embraced BAPS. Akshardham and the Hindu story, only make sense if one hears, and perhaps sings along, the song of bhakti. It is the song that the stones sing next.

Gunatitanand Swami (Aksharbrahma) in bhakti (devotion) to Bhagwan Swaminarayan (Parabrahma) in the central shrine of the Akshardham Mahamandir, depicting the Hindu principle of God along with his ideal devotee, the God-realized guru (*Bhakta sahit Bhagwan*). The bhakta worships Bhagwan while molding oneself after the guru. This bhakti is the foundation of Hinduism.

2

The Song of Bhakti: The Subtle Foundation of Akshardham

WHAT IS BHAKTI?

A young father and his daughter climbed hand in hand up the steps of the mandir in Robbinsville, New Jersey. The young girl's eyes were glued to the approaching murtis in the shrine. She asked her dad, "I understand why Bhagwan (God) is all dressed up, but why did you make me wear my favorite red *kurti* (traditional women's top)? Aren't we here for Bhagwan's darshan?" The father smiled and tapped her on the head. "Well, we are here to see God, but also so that God can see us! We want him to know that we put in the effort. This is how we communicate with God. It is our bhakti. Everything around us in this mandir and everything we do in it. Bhakti is love, darshan, devotion, cooking, speaking, smiling, singing, chanting, dancing, seva." Bhakti is multidimensional. Sages have written hundreds of texts explaining the term. And bhaktas have tried to live it for as many years. **Hindus engage with the Divine and the world through bhakti.**

In Hinduism, God is not abstract or distant, but speaks with you, listens to you. You communicate with the Divine. He accepts your offerings in various forms and shares his blessings for comfort, stability, and spiritual and material growth. The *Narada Bhakti Sutras*, define bhakti as the purest, most giving form of love for the Divine and its creation. Nothing is more valuable on the spiritual path than a personal relationship between Bhagwan and bhakta. **Bhakti, this love, is the seed for the selfless service, inclusivity, open-mindedness, and acceptance that are the hallmark of Hindu spirituality. Bhakti is the bond that holds together people, families, communities—the creation and the creator.**

Hindus also live in the world through the lens of bhakti. Bhagwan Swaminarayan, the founder of the Swaminarayan *Sampraday* (tradition) who is worshipped as a manifestation of the Divine by millions today, favored bhakti. In his canonical text, the Vachanamrut (1829), Bhagwan Swaminarayan explains that one of the foremost markers of love for the Divine is to eat, breathe, and think of God, even while enjoying life. Bhakti is why Hindus balance work, service, play, and spiritual progress.

Bhakti is also why Hindus build mandirs—often majestic, ornate ones—as a symbol of offering one's time, energy, skill,

and wealth to the Divine and the community. These mandirs are centers for ritual, service, and ecumenical growth. Bhakti, then, is the primary reason for building and sharing Akshardham in Robbinsville with the broader Hindu, Indian American, and American community. Understanding bhakti is the first step to understanding Hinduism and this landmark of Hindu faith. The story of Akshardham in New Jersey rests on a foundation of bhakti through murtis, mandirs, and community.

MURTIS AT MANDIRS

Murtis are worshipped and served as the living form of the Divine in Hinduism. *Murti puja* (sacred image worship) is one of the most important modes of ritual and communication with the Divine. In later iterations of Jainism, Buddhism, and other Indic religions, murti puja is one of the fundamental markers of faith and devotion. Murti puja is founded on the belief that God exists and pervades all of creation. That same God makes himself available to bhaktas in the form of a murti, so he can accept their love, prayers, and offerings. This personal relationship with murtis of the Divine is primarily exhibited through *dhyan* (meditation), *prarthana* (prayer), *puja* (ritual worship), *arti* (waving of the sacred lamp), *thal/bhog* (offering food delicacies), *bhajan/kirtan* (singing devotional songs), *abhishek* (ritualistic bathing of murtis) at homes and mandirs.

Murtis can be of varying shapes, sizes, and materials. Sacred texts outline a process for the making of murtis. Murtis are made using specific types of wood, metal, clay, stone, and routinely operate from a position of 'otherness', feeling the need to justify. These mandirs provide them with the opportunity to share more through the architecture, ritual and cultural performances, and sense of community. Second, these mandirs also act as support centers for immigrants and their children adapting to their new homes. Third, the mandir fosters values in families. Parents and children gain tools to bridge the generational gap and respect each other. Finally, and arguably the most important reason for a practicing Hindu, is that a majestic mandir is an offering at the feet of the Divine. It is the ultimate expression of bhakti. This is why Pramukh Swami Maharaj stated at the opening of BAPS Swaminarayan Akshardham, New Delhi in 2005, "We did not build this mandir to show the world or any other religious community that we are better or mightier. It is merely a humble offering at the feet of our guru and God. It is an expression of our bhakti."

BAPS mandirs around the world are built and maintained, physically and financially, primarily by bhaktas and the broader Hindu community as a form of their bhakti. Although these mandirs are bustling with cultural, ritualistic, and humanitarian activities, these mandirs are primarily centers of faith and spiritual centeredness. Young children learn to believe in the Divine and thereby believe in themselves. Young adults are given faith-based tools to face peer pressure and anxiety caused by constant competition and unhealthy comparisons. Parents and adults are taught to take on life with a conviction that the Divine will always give them strength to take on life's crests and troughs.

These faith-based practices prove to be guiding lights in everyday life. This comfort and centeredness are the greatest impact of bhakti through mandirs.

BHAGWAN SWAMINARAYAN AND THE SWAMINARAYAN HINDU COMMUNITY

Mandirs have several murtis, but each mandir is dedicated to one specific deity typically situated in the central shrine. One may see different murtis on a visit to the mandir, and this often confuses the curious non-Hindu visitor. Is Hinduism polytheistic? How many gods are there in Hinduism? The *Rig Veda*, the oldest Hindu sacred text, says, *"Ekam sat vipraha bahudha vadanti"* or *"There is one Truth; the wise speak of It in many ways."* **The short answer is no; Hinduism is not polytheistic. In Hinduism, there is only one God, who manifests in different forms, at different times and places.** Bhaktas may refer to the Divine with different names but there is only one true form of Divinity. Akshardham is dedicated to Bhagwan Swaminarayan (1781–1830), the founder of the Swaminarayan community and worshipped as a manifestation of the Divine by millions. This is his story...

Hindu society, like other religions, adapted to shifting governing bodies, neighboring religious influences, effects of colonial presence, regional cultural influences, and shifting trade and agricultural patterns. As the Mughal Empire crumbled and the British East India Company solidified its hold over parts of the subcontinent, lawlessness, marginalization of certain segments of society, and abuse of power by local rulers, bandits and faux religious godmen were on the rise. It was then, at the turn of the nineteenth century, Bhagwan Swaminarayan founded the Swaminarayan Sampraday within the lineage of bhakti traditions in Hinduism.

Diverse communities and ideological systems have long been a strength of Hinduism. Each one contributed something novel and necessary in the moment of its formation. The practice and belief system that Bhagwan Swaminarayan articulated within the Hindu traditions were a product of his studies of the ancient Hindu scriptures and his interactions with other theologians and the common man across the subcontinent. He founded a community that was embedded in ancient tradition yet was pragmatic and addressed the human predicament in the context of nineteenth-century India. His forward-thinking and progressive ways paved the way for a foundation based on a timeless and universal spirituality.

Bhagwan Swaminarayan was born (manifested) in the small village of Chhapaiya in Uttar Pradesh, which is across the river from one of Hinduism's most renowned pilgrimage sites: Ayodhya. He renounced his home at the age of eleven and traveled across the Indian subcontinent to study the reality of his time and bless seekers. After observing and learning from various communities and faiths, he settled in Gujarat, in the western region of India. He wove together a community of faithful from varied backgrounds. His focus on ethics, social equality and inclusion, and a respect for tradition embedded in the age-old traditions of Hindu Sanatan Dharma earned him praise from his contemporaries. This inherent sense of social inclusiveness awed British and local rulers.

He initiated more than 2500 sadhus who dedicated their lives to serving society. His order of celibate sadhus battled superstition, repressive customs, addiction, and fear through blind faith to empower aspirants to find their own path to the Divine. These sadhus raised awareness about mutual respect, personal hygiene and sanitation, amd education and literacy for men and women. They brought about a resurgence in the arts, literature, music, and architecture. Bhagwan Swaminarayan's cultural renaissance resulted in the creation of hundreds of literary texts in various languages and more than 25,000 bhakti poems. Brahmanand Swami, Premanand Swami, Nishkulanand Swami, Muktanand Swami, and Devanand Swami were his foremost bhakti-poet-musician sadhus. They revived the temple music and literary tradition and are celebrated all over India for their contributions.

Bhagwan Swaminarayan built mandirs as centers for spiritual and social development. These mandirs served as centers for social reform and humanitarian service during famines and natural disasters. They were not just stone structures, but rather living centers of love and service that could affect change in people's lives and thereby change society, one family at a time.

All these great contributions culminated in the experience that people had with his inherent Divinity. His presence brought comfort and an inner satisfaction only experienced in the presence of the Divine. Two million people revered Bhagwan Swaminarayan as God manifest on Earth during his lifetime and millions more came to revere him in the two centuries after his passing away in 1830. His ability to emanate this divinity while remaining accessible set him apart in the minds of millions.

In the Vachanamrut, Bhagwan Swaminarayan highlighted several key messages. First, he instructed his bhaktas to live a morally-pure and value-based life. He instructed his bhaktas to avoid the four major sins: theft, intoxication, violence, and adultery. This decorum would strengthen the social fabric. He instructed his bhaktas to search for the *atman* (the inner self; soul within). Realizing the strength of the atman was the key to embracing the trials and tribulations of life with stability and ease. He encouraged his bhaktas to overcome their sense of "I" and selflessly serve society without any expectations or desires. He instructed them to find a God-realized guru and learn to grow at the guru's feet. A God-realized guru who was in constant communion with the Divine was pivotal to transcending the human condition.

Bhagwan Swaminarayan also gave practical spiritual advice that would reform society. He instructed his bhaktas and others in Gujarat to stop the practice of *sati* or burning the widow on her husband's funeral pyre. He stopped female infanticide and the custom of dowry. Bhagwan Swaminarayan also founded the first girls' school in Gujarat. He instructed all bhaktas to treat women with respect and value their contributions to the household and workforce. He motivated his devotees to donate five or ten percent of their income in goods or currency as seva to the mandirs. These funds were used to give back to the community through humanitarian seva and development programs.

Bhagwan Swaminarayan also emphasized a code of conduct for his devotees regarding dietary restrictions and personal spiritual practices. Similar to Vaishnava traditions within Hinduism, Swaminarayan bhaktas follow a strict lacto-vegetarian diet while avoiding *tamasic* and *rajasic* (dull or arousing) foods such as onion and garlic. Bhaktas are taught to offer their meals to God before a murti or through meditation prior to having their meals. Swaminarayan bhaktas have a consistent morning prayer ritual (*nitya puja*), which is performed after bathing. Furthermore, Swaminarayan bhaktas wear *tulsi* (basil-wood) beads around their neck as a sign of their faith and submission. Male bhaktas also apply a tilak-chandlo and female bhaktas apply a *chandlo* on their forehead every morning.

Finally, Bhagwan Swaminarayan instructed his devotees to love and respect people regardless of the religious, sectarian, social, caste-based, or economic differences between them. Bhagwan Swaminarayan's greatest innovation in the bhakti world was to work against the disparaging effects of the caste system. He won the hearts of millions who had gone unheard and unnoticed. (Bhagwan Swaminarayan's efforts to integrate society are discussed in further detail in Chapter 4.) It was this foundational aspect of spirituality that shaped the way in which his community came to see people, living beings, and nature. Environmentalism, conservation, equality, and inclusion all stemmed from this spiritual principle in the Swaminarayan community. This, in turn, came to shape the social landscape of modern India and the Indian diaspora.

He showed his followers that bhakti is the foundation for how Hindus live, learn, love, and serve the world. Over the past 250 years, Swaminarayan bhaktas have persevered to live this bhakti lifestyle prescribed by Bhagwan Swaminarayan.

BHAKTI AT AKSHARDHAM

What is bhakti then? It is how Hindus engage with the world around them and communicate directly with its creator and sustainer. Bhakti, in all its complexities and joy, comes full circle at Akshardham.

There are several common expressions of bhakti that visitors may observe at Akshardham. First, do not be surprised if you notice bhaktas touching each other's feet (*namaskar* or *pranam*), or if a young member of the community approaches you and bows to touch your feet. They are bowing to the Divine within you. Visitors may also notice pilgrims and bhaktas offering incense sticks (*dhup* or *agarbatti*) to the towering, golden murti of Nilkanth Varni as a sign of devotion and prayer. Many bhaktas perform *dandvats* (prostration by laying one's body on the floor as a sign of submission to the Divine) and *pradakshinas* (circumambulations) in front of the murtis in the mandir. Bhaktas may be participating in the mandir ritual of abhishek. Finally, arti and thal/bhog are common rituals at any Hindu mandir. Sadhus and priests wave a sacred lamp in front of the murtis to facilitate the viewing of the murti for bhaktas several times a day at a mandir. They also offer food offerings several times a day to the murtis. If you partake in the arti ritual, you may be asked to sit according to the mandir's practices. If you eat a food item during your visit to Akshardham, it is likely you are tasting food offered to and sanctified by the deities. Finally, bhajan/kirtan (bhakti song) and *katha* (spiritual discourse) are spiritual nourishment for the soul. You may see bhaktas singing in front of the murtis or listening to spiritual discourses at any given time at Akshardham.

Bhakti, then, is everything in the world through the lens of love, service, inclusivity, participation, and devotion. Akshardham is one such mandir that brings it all together on a grand scale for the community at large to experience. Understanding bhakti, murtis, and mandirs in the Hindu context is a critical primer to Akshardham in Robbinsville. **As compelling and majestic as this stone structure appears, the guiding principle of why mandirs exist and what makes them possible is as soft as love.** The rituals, spiritual counseling, devotional performances, and artistic creations create an environment that not only provides a space for Hindus to feel at home, but also for them to share their culture and rituals with their local community. It is this sense of pride and comfort which empowers them to serve selflessly. This selfless service is the most outward expression of bhakti, and it is what makes the mandir possible. It is the song which the stones sing next.

Seva (selfless service) is the most visible form of bhakti at Akshardham. One selflessly serves to transcend the human condition. From polishing and waterproofing the stones to serving the local community during humanitarian crises, BAPS volunteers serve without desire for reward or recognition.

3

The Song of Seva: The Steps to Akshardham

―◆◆◆―

SEVA: BEYOND VOLUNTEERISM

There is an ancient Upanishadic (from the end part of the Vedas) tale that most children hear growing up in a Hindu household. A young boy, Satyakam, goes to a spiritual master seeking enlightenment. He wants to realize his inner self and the Divine. His guru lends him a herd of 400 cattle and tells him to return when there are 1,000. Enlightenment would find him. How, when, and with what guarantees? This was unknown to the boy. He bows to his guru and goes to the forest. He returns and now knows "something" that he did not know before—something within. This story captures a few of the foundational principles of seva—faith and trust, effort and sincerity, humility, and, most importantly, dissolving one's sense of "I". The boy served selflessly, thereby realizing his inner self and transcending the human condition.

There is a glaring question that troubles the first-time listener: "Who serves without expectation of reward or acknowledgment these days?" The answer is, "No one." But people do serve, and they always have—in America, in India, around the world. Volunteers serve to fill the gaps in society when and where governance and commerce fall short. As Americans, previous leaders have often reminded us to "ask what you can do for your country" before asking "what your country can do for you." This call to American civic duty is an important part of the Indian American identity.

Volunteerism plays an important function in faith-based communities too. In the Indic traditions, Sikhs, Jains, Buddhists, and Hindus have all emphasized the need to serve to transcend. Das Kabir, a famous North-Indian bhakti poet celebrated by Hindus, Sikhs and Muslims, sings, "One and all stand tall and stroll proud. Not one cares to bend. But if one merely bends [and serves], one shall rise above the rest."

What is this "bending" that Kabir speaks of? It goes beyond what we tend to understand as volunteerism. **Seva in the broadest sense can be translated as selfless service—without expectation, recognition, or concern for comfort and convenience.** In seva, one chooses to forget the sense of external self and transcends ego to serve the Divine, the spiritual master, and all of creation. **Seva is not merely service; it is the passionate, proactive desire to serve selflessly.** If bhakti is how Hindus engage with and see the world, seva is how Hindus act and do in the world. **If bhakti is why mandirs are, seva is how mandirs come to be. Seva is a** functional manifestation of bhakti. Seva is the way to ascend the steps, to transcend, at Akshardham.

Though the benefits of seva may seem to be a cost savings or momentum-generating exercise for building a religious complex, operating faith-based schools, or organizing humanitarian initiatives, this perspective changes when one witnesses it and participates firsthand—when one hears the songs of the stones. **Akshardham is a product of the seva culture uniquely cultivated with Hindu values and American civic duty within the BAPS Swaminarayan community.** Here is what the stones sing of selfless service as a distinctively Swaminarayan Hindu-American song.

SEVA WITHIN THE SWAMINARAYAN HINDU TRADITION: BY GOD AND GURU

Seva or volunteerism for the BAPS Swaminarayan Sanstha is not one of its central activities or initiatives; in reality, it is its only "activity" and at once its modus operandi. Seva has a unique position within the Swaminarayan tradition. In the Vachanamrut, Bhagwan Swaminarayan praises one of his bhaktas, "Just as Uka Khachar has become addicted to selfless service, in the same way, if one becomes addicted to serving God and guru to the extent that one would not be able to stay for even a moment without serving them, then all of the impure desires within shall be destroyed." **Serving society is a primary way to reach the Divine, a path to enlightenment. Seva then leads to moksha, the ultimate spiritual state.** Furthermore, in the Swaminarayan tradition, the desire and the opportunity to serve endlessly *is* that state of release. Seva is moksha.

Bhagwan Swaminarayan's own actions and those inspired in his sadhus and followers made seva an integral part of the organization's core theology, work ethos, and identity. Most importantly, Bhagwan Swaminarayan encouraged service and worship in a way that inspired unity. Seva is a way to come together—to forget where one comes from and celebrate where one is and what is being created. There are dozens of documented examples in the tradition's sacred texts in which Bhagwan Swaminarayan himself served alongside his sadhus and bhaktas from all backgrounds, such as to dig water reservoirs or carry stones to construction sites. Sadhus, kings, chieftains, merchants, and farmers all served side by side. He encouraged privileged members of society to serve the needy and marginalized. He promoted the integration of those from the marginalized segments of society. **Bhagwan Swaminarayan's mode of seva acted as a catalyst to bring society together.**

This culture of seva continued. From building mandirs and schools, to educating children and integrating marginalized communities, and to even caring for livestock and water bodies, Bhagwan Swaminarayan and the Swaminarayan tradition became one of several distinguished Hindu communities for organizing and implementing a dedicated and skilled volunteer force. **Somewhat like the way Sikhs sedimented seva in their religious practice, the Swaminarayan community was founded, and later proliferated, on the bedrock of seva.**

Bhagwan Swaminarayan's fifth spiritual successor, Pramukh Swami Maharaj, too, served by example. He took his personal desire to serve and formulated it into the organization's work ethos like never before. He took every opportunity to serve, whether it be through action or intent. Even after becoming the guru and the president of the organization, he was often caught by disciples cleaning bathrooms, scrubbing floors, and picking up used dental sticks outside public restrooms in his own mandirs. He would take every opportunity to help a lone sadhu roll out carts of trash and serve food morsels to his disciples when they were unwell.

Most impressive of all was his intent to serve despite his old age and frail health. Following the Gujarat Earthquake of 2001, Pramukh Swami Maharaj frequently called his bhaktas and sadhus in Bhuj late at night to follow up on the day's relief effort tasks. He reminded them to serve the victims of the earthquake in the way they would serve Bhagwan Swaminarayan. And that is why one night, he woke up in the middle of the night and called one of the sadhus to remind him to include nail clippers in the relief kits to restore a sense of normalcy for the victims. This genuine care and understanding for those in need was a marker of his seva. This became the golden standard for seva in BAPS from the 1970s to this current moment in time.

SEVA BY BAPS AND BAPS CHARITIES

The sophistication of the BAPS volunteer organization only strengthened with time. It truly blossomed into a globally recognized force under Pramukh Swami Maharaj, when international aid organizations and state and federal governments started asking BAPS and BAPS Charities to partner with them and execute humanitarian initiatives following pandemics, and organizing healthcare drives. The volunteers come from such diverse professional and skilled backgrounds that they can take on a wide variety of tasks such as mandir construction, healthcare, educational activities, environmental support, cultural programs, and even legal and technical services. **Combining this dedication, valuable experience, and pool of able volunteers enables the organization to effect change in communities around the world.**

There is a sophisticated volunteer coordination system in the organization. Despite this structure, each volunteer is willing to take on any task they are prescribed. No one feels too privileged or too smart for the greater good that can come from service being performed. Impressively, these volunteers do not have a cap on the amount of time they contribute. Many of these volunteers dedicate dozens of hours a week despite balancing demanding professional careers and healthy social lives.

In seva, the clarity of purpose and intention is key. BAPS has an impeccable track record of working on monumental spiritual and humanitarian projects around the world. The institution operates as a conduit through which members of society can serve the underserved and needy around the world. Several surgeons, urban planning experts, and lawyers have provided service to underprivileged immigrants and communities through BAPS' initiatives. It is for these reasons that notable lawmakers, heads of state, and local community leaders have commended BAPS' initiatives to serve society. Mohamed Al Khaja, the first UAE Ambassador to Israel, lauded the professionalism and spirit of the BAPS volunteer corps by recommending that they train and inspire locals in the UAE to serve with a similar connection with humans.

For BAPS volunteers, it is not just the number of activities or even the level of impact. It is the focus on people, families, and communities. It is not to further the name of the organization or its guru nor expand outward. It is to strengthen from within— to become better individuals and to advance on the path to moksha. **Every BAPS volunteer aims to be a 'Satyakam' and achieve enlightenment through selfless service as prescribed by the guru.** Most of them just do not have to do it with a herd of cattle in the forest.

SEVA'S SONG AT AKSHARDHAM IN NEW JERSEY

Seva at Akshardham is unique, even within the BAPS context. Though this is not completely different from other mandirs built by BAPS around the world, this was the first time that more than 12,500 volunteers put their lives on hold from anywhere between two weeks to twelve years for the construction of a house of worship. Many of them took a leave of absence from their work, some even quit their jobs and sold their businesses, others sold their homes, and several moved cross-country to ensure the completion of the mandir. The building and maintenance of

Akshardham is an exemplar of the guiding principle of seva that has become the organizational identity of BAPS.

Imagine: nearly 75 percent of the entire campus is designed, constructed, managed, and maintained by sadhus and volunteers. At Akshardham in North America, most of what one sees, from the construction to executive management, all have the hand of a volunteer somewhere in the process. Even those tasks for which professional help was hired beyond the manpower or specific skills of the available volunteer force, the ancillary support is always provided by the volunteers of the community. This includes everything from architectural design to the cleaning of the facilities. These contributions allow for the organization to use the community's monetary and in-kind donations prudently.

And that spirit of service is infectious. Many of the consultants who started off as fully hired vendors and contractors too gave hundreds of hours and in-kind donations in service. Several of the contractors who were hired for structural engineering and traffic engineering put in extra hours without expecting recognition. They worked with a passion in support of a project that they came to regard as their own.

THREE FORMS OF SEVA AT AKSHARDHAM

Three principal modes of seva are apparent in the Swaminarayan tradition, and specifically at Akshardham. **First and foremost, there are those who serve physically (***tan***).** There is always something to do for everyone, from serving cool, spiced lemonade to chiseling away at the stones for the Akshardham Mahamandir.

These volunteers perform each task irrelevant to their own background. Accomplished business owners collected and compacted trash and waste from the construction site. Reputed physicians from New York City and neighboring counties visited every Tuesday to polish stones. Young mothers and middle-aged grandmothers reinforced concrete with rebar, as even younger college students organized the numbered stones for reassembly.

BAPS volunteers commit different levels of time and energy. Some dedicate hours or days per month. Some have even decided to volunteer for the rest of their lives. Some prefer to volunteer their skill or time but may be unable to afford the associated expenses. The community contributes to their service-related expenses so that they can support their families and livelihoods while serving society. Many more contribute their skills and resources, only accepting enough to live a modest life in the process. Each of these seva models are respected and appreciated within the community.

The second form of service is financial and in-kind donations (*dhan*). A general misconception about BAPS is that it grows through governmental grants, corporate sponsorships, and donations from business magnates. In the case of BAPS, and especially in the case of Akshardham, it is quite the opposite. The donations provided by the middle- and lower-middle class bhaktas have a major impact on the completion of the project. It is important to remember that financial contributions within the community are not seen as a means to gain access or favor. These donations are seva of the Divine and seen as a way of giving back to the community. These funds are collected by senior bhaktas and sadhus in the community, who sometimes refuse to accept donations. They advise devotees to balance their passion and tenacity to serve with the responsibilities of their family and household. There is room for everyone to give in a way that is appropriate and convenient given their financial means. In-kind supplies are also donated for humanitarian or social initiatives, such as food, sanitary products, education and healthcare machinery, and building products. Seva is not meant to complicate matters in the bhaktas' lives. The guru sees the bhaktas as his children and takes the responsibility of their well-being and long-term financial planning upon his shoulders. This balance between giving and receiving underpins the financial and in-kind seva at Akshardham.

The final mode of giving comes in the form of prayer and intent—a mindfulness in the form of care (*man*). Prayer is perhaps the most vital form of seva. *Prarthana* (a heartfelt prayer to Bhagwan) is said to be one of the most effective ways of assisting others. When asked if they need anything, Hindus will often ask their family members or friends to "pray for me." Mahant Swami Maharaj asked the sadhus and bhaktas to pray for the completion of Akshardham as their most important contribution. Prayer also reminds the bhakta that Bhagwan is the all-doer. He or she is just serving.

There are also those who serve with their **words**, by speaking of the complex and the tradition to those who visit, to their neighbors, and to the curious within the community. One should not confuse this with proselytization; rather, it is sharing information about Akshardham and Hinduism without wanting to convert or impress their views upon others. Hindus have been a bit reticent to speak about their faith to others. As stated earlier, there was a sense of foreignness that they felt in relation to the world's religions. These differences led them to remain quiet and practice their faith without speaking openly about it in America. This form of seva is a means to address that silence and to clear any misconceptions that people around them may have. Serving through pleasant thoughts and words helps one increase tolerance and faith in the community.

For those who cannot do that, there is seva through **intent**. Wanting to serve and intending to support even if it is from a distance, in silence and with inaction, the seva is registered with the Divine and the guru. **Seva at its core is not just an outward act. Seva is desiring to do good as well. This is what earns the pleasure of the guru and the Divine on the spiritual journey.** In fact, anyone and everyone who serves physically, financially, and with their words and thoughts, must also serve through intent. Another important part of serving with the mind is to serve in a way that increases positivity in the community. No amount of action or charity can earn the pleasure of the guru and the Divine unless it is done with a flavor of positivity, regard for others, and the intent to unite.

AKSHARDHAM AS A PLATFORM FOR SEVA

Most of the community's day to day operations at a house of worship and cultural center are also run by volunteers, from cultural classes to spiritual counseling, from the feeding of thousands every week to the design and production of outreach and learning programs. Volunteers also serve passionately in the local Robbinsville and New Jersey community (Chapter 5). Their service reached far beyond Akshardham and their local community.

The volunteers from the BAPS Robbinsville community have also served globally. Following the 2021 earthquake in Haiti, they sent considerable funds and resources to help rebuild the island nation's infrastructure. One of the most ambitious and timely service operations was a humanitarian trip to Poland and the Ukrainian border at the start of the Russia-Ukraine War in 2022. Several of the community's young men joined a troop of BAPS volunteers from Europe to help refugees lawfully cross into Poland and find stability as they were fleeing Ukraine during the first month of the war. Six volunteers from the community in New Jersey flew to Poland in a matter of hours. Dozens more worked with the local community to raise funds and in-kind donations for the people of Ukraine in these border towns in Poland. One of the volunteers from Robbinsville was a recent father who left behind his wife and five-month-old baby to serve those who needed his presence even more. When asked, Dharmik Sheth reminded the reporters and a local Congressman, "I did not serve there for recognition or a thrill. It was something that I observed as a child. Seva is the core of my *sadhana* (spiritual journey). I was called to serve in Ukraine. I will go wherever I am asked to serve. I do not want or deserve credit. I want to give in the way that my guru has given his whole life." Equally noteworthy are the contributions of his wife, Meera Sheth, who stayed behind and enabled her husband to serve. Their story inspired dozens from the tri-state area to follow in their footsteps and serve in Poland and Ukraine during the early stages of the war, when local municipalities and international aid organizations were scrambling to set up infrastructure for refugees.

For the Sheths, and thousands of families like them, seva is the means to transcend the human condition and become one with the Divine. People have experienced a sense of fulfillment within that allows them to take on their own anxiety, anger, and greed. **Seva works to lessen the effects of the sense of "I", and thereby progress on the spiritual journey. Seva molds brighter minds, purer hearts, and realized souls.** This spiritual reward is why people choose to serve at Akshardham. Peace and satisfaction are their only expectations.

When seva becomes the way of life, it creates an environment of generosity and acceptance. People are not expected or instructed to serve and give; rather they want to give, and they also inspire others to give. When this becomes the norm, bhakti and seva come together in this setting to change the way one sees the world and acts in it. This leads to a refined sense of being—the making of a new person inside and out. The stones' next song is of these exemplary humans—the bhaktas.

These distinctly-colored hard hats represent the 12,500 volunteers—men, women, sadhus, and skilled artisan volunteers–who came together to build the Mahamandir. The foundational principles of bhakti and seva are lived at Akshardham: seeing the Divine in all, inclusivity, personal and spiritual growth, and enthusiasm and dedication.

4

The Song of Bhaktas: The Pillars of Akshardham

BHAKTI + SEVA = BHAKTA

Even before a visitor is greeted by the serene glow of the golden murti of Nilkanth Varni or the sky-skimming spire of the Mahamandir at Akshardham, one first encounters the living representation of bhakti and seva: the bhakta. Bhakta, here, is used in the broadest sense of the word. One does not have to be a Swaminarayan Hindu to be a bhakta. A bhakta embodies the principles of bhakti and seva. A bhakta serves while experiencing the Divine in all those around him or her. A bhakta aims to selflessly serve and love.

Whether it is a parking and security volunteer at the front gate or a landscape specialist tending to the Japanese maples on campus, they all have one thing in common: they wear a smile. This smile is not a corporate tool or a forced publicity tactic. This smile is rooted in the bliss experienced through a nurturing environment.

This smile is powered by the spiritual momentum derived from bhakti and seva. **If bhakti is why and how Hindus engage with the world, and seva is how they act in the world, the synergy of both is how they are in the world.** It exudes a sense of personal centeredness, communal inclusivity, and collective enthusiasm.

The first part of this chapter describes the culture through which bhakti and seva are performed at Akshardham—the central melodies of the stories to come. The second part echoes the stones' songs of the bhaktas' experiences. These bhaktas and their stories are the pillars of Akshardham.

INCLUSIVITY AND RESPECT

Bhakti encourages universal acceptance and respect of people regardless of their social and financial station in society. This inspires a world without division—a world without corners. Love and service enable people to build bridges across religious, social, and economic barriers.

Despite these ideals of unity and inclusion, marginalization via hierarchy and exclusion crept into a rigid social structure within societies around the world, including in India. India's ancient social order was meant to be a fluid system that allowed for mobility of individuals and a shifting scale of import for entire *varnas* (social class). Unfortunately, that system came to be tainted over time by those within society who were hoarding power and later through colonial rule who found it beneficial for governance to prescribe permanent labels to people, leading to long-term subjugation of entire communities. It was as if people lived in separate and unequal spheres. Over time, important social elements such as respect, empathy, and generosity eroded, and the *varna* and *jati* or caste system emerged as a power structure which marginalized entire communities. Similar to the divisions in America and Europe caused by race, ethnic origins, religion, political ideology, and economic means, it would take many strong reformers and forces to work together and realign society after hundreds of years of division and oppression.

Many beacons of hope tried to unify society. They taught important lessons of open-mindedness, which served as a model for members in the community. In India, at the turn of the nineteenth century, Bhagwan Swaminarayan was one such beacon in Gujarat, India. His social reform work in western India caught the attention of community leaders from within the Hindu tradition as well as the British colonial rulers. He persevered to integrate and empower the most marginalized communities in Indian society, namely the Dalit (Scheduled Class) and Adivasi (Scheduled Tribe). These members of society were often called "untouchables" and treated in grotesque ways. Bhagwan Swaminarayan did not just restore their access to temple rituals and worship, but also visited their homes—ate with them and lived with them.

His sadhus and bhaktas followed in his footsteps bringing about a social revolution that would shape western India and the diaspora for the next two centuries by promoting social integration, women's education and equality, and mutual respect between religious communities. Two important British historians, William Hodge Mill and Bishop Reginald Heber, have noted that

Bhagwan Swaminarayan had disciples from all varnas and that he integrated them into his community. The scholars note that these distinctions of social order were mere "cardinal ordinance," and that Bhagwan Swaminarayan "taught his disciples that they should look for judgment according to their works and actions, not according to birth." In fact, he even took diverse followers from his community, including a Muslim and a Dalit follower, to meet the British Governor of Bombay, Sir John Malcolm, on 28 February 1830. He practiced what he preached and ate with and lived in the homes of Dalits and Adivasis, those most marginalized in Indian society, to set an example of integration and inclusion that changed the Indian landscape forever.

Pramukh Swami Maharaj continued this wave of reform at an even faster and bolder pace. Like Bhagwan Swaminarayan, the guru advocated for the upliftment of these ostracized communities and provided them with resources needed to integrate into urban society, access modern education institutions, and maintain healthy lifestyles. He had a longing to see, hear, and love those who the rest of society did not dare "touch." He was one of the first Hindu gurus to break all barriers of caste in sadhu initiation when he initiated the first members of certain varnas into the saffron garb in 1981. Mahant Swami Maharaj embedded this principle into one of the canonical texts of the community, the *Satsang Diksha* (2020). He writes that caste, gender, and creed have no effect on one's ability to transcend spiritually. One's true form is the atman and not this body. The soul has no external social markers. In essence, when bhakti and seva come together they do not leave room for discrimination or mistreatment, ever.

In the American context, the bhakta plays an important role in building bridges between people from the Indian American community and those with whom he or she interacts within a professional, social, or mandir setting. Race, religion, ethnicity, and gender are but external markers that are respected but looked past when it comes to connecting with someone. This is not to say that a person's identity is not respected and catered to, but that the bhakta looks to love and serve alongside others without fixating on these differences. The building of Akshardham is a story of unity and collaboration at the core. Like earlier bhakti networks in India and around the world, Akshardham brought together a wide variety of people during its making. Sadhus, bhaktas, consultants, contractors, and vendors of different backgrounds came together to give back for generations to come.

GROWING THROUGH BHAKTI AND SEVA

An equally important theme that resonates from the stories of the bhaktas is that of personal growth—both professional and spiritual. Thousands of bhaktas gained new skill sets while serving at Akshardham. The list of professional skills is vast. College students and recent graduates benefited from a head start in soft skill development and human interaction in the working environment. Young professionals were entrusted with the management of technological integration and traditional construction. And finally, many retired and senior volunteers found renewed utility of their knowhow through mentorship of young volunteers. **This process of growth fosters collaboration over competition. Bhaktas serve side by side, to give—not to take.** The scale of this volunteer collaboration is beyond impressive. **Over the last 15 years, more than 12,500 volunteers physically served together in different capacities.**

Spiritual growth can be tangibly measured by how one *is* in this world. Becoming a version of oneself that is pleasant and at ease, eventually achieving an inner equilibrium, or *stithapragyata*, is a marker of spirituality. Shri Krishna Bhagwan makes note of this in the second chapter of his *Shrimad Bhagavad Gita*. **This sense of stability is at the center of almost every tale of the bhakta's progress.** This achievement is gifted by the Divine through bhakti and seva at Akshardham.

This genuine desire to progress spiritually fuels the volunteerism at Akshardham. Many volunteers are vocal about how they are driven by the desire for moksha through seva. They also express a desire to conquer anger, greed, lust, envy, and attachment. They serve selflessly so that they can transcend the human condition, find steadiness and comfort within, and experience a sense of constant union with the Divine. There are also those who may not explicitly articulate this desire for spiritual transcendence, but they express it through feelings of comfort within and a lifestyle free from anxiety. **Countless youngsters have spoken of their ability to tune out negativity and attract positivity through service.**

The bhaktas' desire to serve continuously at Akshardham is evidence of this feeling of self-growth and inner satisfaction. The end goal is not to be released from seva, but to desire more opportunities to serve, and to enjoy them.

ENTHUSIASM AND DEDICATION

Enthusiasm and dedication overwhelm those visiting Akshardham. In BAPS, bhaktas often show more enthusiasm for their service at the Akshardham complex and for the organization over their own full-time, paying day-jobs. This passion is rooted in the bhakta's love for culture, faith, and affecting positive change in society. Often the volunteers, too, look back and wonder how they were able to serve so selflessly. *Samarpan* is a word used often in the context of sevá. Samarpan is a unique blend of sacrifice and submission. The English words do not quite capture the flavor of the Indic term. Sacrifice imagines giving something up. Submission implies offering yourself to another and tends to skew negatively. **In samarpan, one does not quite sacrifice or submit—one just gives because they love and want to serve.** The seva of bhaktas at Akshardham is defined by this samarpan. **They give limitlessly because they love.** The bhaktas are driven by their love for the Divine and its creation—by their love for the guru. This love can move mountains. This foundational principle allows people to give with tenacity while also remaining accommodating of others. It truly is a unique phenomenon and can be difficult to fathom for those unfamiliar with the concept of bhakti and seva.

THE BHAKTAS: THE PILLARS OF AKSHARDHAM

The bhaktas are the pillars of Akshardham—they bear its weight and at once enhance its beauty. These brief introductions are not meant to impress, but are meant to inspire positivity in the lives of those who hear these songs.

FULL STOMACHS, FULLER HEARTS

Savita Patel and her husband, Soma Patel, had previously purchased a beachfront townhome in Hawaii. Retirement was going to be great in this picturesque setting. When they heard that the construction of the Akshardham complex was about to begin, they changed their lifelong plans and moved to Central Jersey. There is a Gujarati colloquialism, "Worship the stomach first. One can then effortlessly worship the Divine and its creation." Savita knew how food motivated and united people. And that is why, in 2012, Savita undertook the task of making food and spiced chai for the volunteers full-time.

Savita's chai would warm the hearts of hundreds of volunteers over the next decade. She and her husband arrive at the mandir at 6:45 a.m. and stay until 3:30 p.m. Despite undergoing two knee replacement surgeries in 2016 and 2019 and bearing the loss of one of her children over the last decade, Savita continues to brew her trademark chai and serve daily in the kitchen. Many of the volunteers who go back home after serving at Akshardham, often regard the now 80-year-old, loving figure as their "mother" in Robbinsville.

A FAMILY THAT SERVES TOGETHER...

Taru Patel watched her husband, Vinod Patel, pack his suitcase. She had seen him do it countless times. Per their usual routine, she reviewed the simple contents of the bag to ensure he had packed what he needed and then offered a supportive smile.

Vinod left his first job to serve in the building of mandirs, most notably the Akshardham Mahamandirs in Gandhinagar (1992) and New Delhi (2005) and the renowned BAPS Shri Swaminarayan Mandir in London (1995). After years of seva in India, Vinod moved to America with his wife and two children in 2003. His family was ecstatic. They had lived a middle-class life in urban India. Now was their chance to settle in America and make the most of their dreams. He hoped to find a job and get settled swiftly. The first call he received for "work" was a call to serve.

Over time, Vinod was requested to settle on the small Greek island of Thasos. His was not the experience of a holiday that Thasos is known for today. Thasos is also known for its marble quarries. Amidst the backdrop of a foreign land with a language that Vinod did not speak, he toiled at those quarry sites from dawn to dusk, after which he returned to his room and often prepared a simple porridge with rice and lentils in the pressure cooker he had brought from home. He jumped around from quarry to quarry and even traveled as far as Turkey and Bulgaria by car to secure marble and limestone. Vinod spent about six-and-a-half years on that island, away from his family and away from the comforts of home, until all the required stone had been excavated and shipped to India for testing and carving. Beyond his seva for Akshardham, Vinod grew to be celebrated by the island's residents for routinely volunteering to help the elderly buy groceries, fix their small appliances, and drive them around to complete errands. Once a sevak, always a sevak!

Meanwhile, Taru singlehandedly managed the household, worked part-time, and raised their children. A senior sadhu once remarked, "The only people who deserve more credit than Vinod are his wife and kids. Truly a family effort to serve." The family reflects on that time with a smile—they fondly recall the consequences of their seva because of the closeness, inner satisfaction, and growth they achieved together as a family, despite the geographic distance.

"NO TEA BREAKS FOR ME."

Before he got on the flight to America, Satish Jangid had hardly traveled outside of his home district in Rajasthan. Maybe twice—once when he traveled to meet his guru, Pramukh Swami Maharaj, in Gujarat, and the other time when he traveled to New Delhi to get his American visas. He had heard so much about *pardesh* (the foreign land). He could hardly believe that he was getting the opportunity to build a Hindu mandir in America. Satish comes from a community of skilled stone and wood craftsmen. They are referred to as *shilpis* (sculptors) or as 'Vishvakarmas' after the celestial Hindu deity of architecture. Once thought to be a dying art, the community has benefitted greatly from the renaissance of traditional mandir architecture attributed to organizations such as BAPS.

If you catch Satish instructing a group of sadhus or volunteers on how to work with a stone pillar or install a carved statuette, you will immediately observe his beaming smile and the lightness with which he carries himself. You may also notice that he declines the ever-popular tea break. When asked why, he explained, "I do not want to lose out on my opportunity to serve and grow. Ask my wife if you ever go to Hindua, Rajasthan. I have come a long way. My anger and easily irritable nature have taken a turn for the better since I started serving at mandirs. I cannot explain it. I have just changed, and it has changed my marriage and family life."

Satish first traveled to the United States during the building of the BAPS Shri Swaminarayan Mandir in Houston, Texas in the early 2000s. He has been serving in Robbinsville since 2016. He never misses the two early morning arti rituals at 6:00 am and then at 7:30 am at the mandir. Satish views his volunteer work at Akshardham as an opportunity for seva.

Satish's story is one of the most powerful ones for it combines his enthusiasm for service with his desire to better himself. He was not born into a Swaminarayan family but was drawn to the faith through seva. His story is certainly a compelling one, but it is not an anomaly. Many have donated years of their life to serve. If you happen to run into Satish on your visit, do ask him about his passion for cooking. He makes spicy Rajasthani dishes enjoyed by many of the volunteers from all over America who serve alongside him—a seva family that laughs, eats, and serves together.

THE POWER OF THE ATMAN

Dipna Patel spent the first few years after marriage commuting back and forth from Massachusetts to Cherry Hill, New Jersey, where her husband lived. She was finishing graduate school. She was excited about starting a new life with her husband. And then this happened.

Her husband was quiet in the car. She sensed his hesitation. She asked if everything was okay. He had been thinking about the request to serve at Akshardham. "I want to serve. Full-time. We might have to put our life on hold for a bit longer. I need your blessings to start. It won't be easy, but when are we going to get to be a part of such a seva project again?" He had taken the words right out of her mouth. She agreed enthusiastically.

There was, however, a small problem. Dipna doubted if she had the physical strength to serve. She derived the physical and mental strength from the spiritual bedrock of Hinduism—*atmajnan* (the realization of the atman or inner self). She reminded herself that her true inner self was the soul, not the body. It helped her. She had always thought of this as a theoretical aspect of Hinduism. She now understood that pain, trouble, and struggles could all be faced with ease through this one seminal thought. Seva helped her realize the atman.

Her seva did not end there. Her husband's friend from the community in Munster, Indiana, left his job and joined the seva in Robbinsville. He moved in with them and would commute with Dipna's husband every morning for seva. He lived with them for over a year, and eventually his wife and child also moved in with them. It seemed like a natural addition to the family. When asked if it was difficult, Dipna shared, "Why would it be? He is my brother too. We are family—connected by the bond of seva."

A SEVAK EXECUTIVE

A senior executive in the organization can be seen daily on the mandir campus in a simple, crisp shirt and pleated pants—always neat and yet austere. His trademark greeting to anyone is the standard bowing salutation, except that he makes it a point to touch the feet of every passing volunteer and bhakta, senior or not. As a leading executive and senior devotee, he is respected by sadhus and volunteers. Though in his late 60s, he walks with a spring in his step, almost as if he is enthused with the spirit of service and is willing to take on any task.

This volunteer ascended the corporate ladder as an executive while also dedicating an average of 35 hours a week as a youth coordinator and volunteer for cultural programs, and even maintenance and housekeeping of the first BAPS mandir in Flushing, New York. No seva was too small. Over the years, he emerged as a leader because of his commitment to seva, respect for others, and inward eye for spiritual progress. He was entrusted with even more responsibilities as the organization grew in America. In the early 2000s, he left his job and joined the organization as a full-time volunteer.

He turned his attention to the Akshardham project. He operated alongside a team of young professional volunteers and willingly accepted their reverse mentorship. He did all of this with the support of his family. His wife worked night shifts as a supervisor in a laboratory to help financially. Despite her full-time job, his wife also contributed nearly three dozen hours of service in the communal kitchen every week.

On his journey to serve, he found a way to balance achieving results and growing from within. This is best illustrated by his dedication to physical service amid all his executive responsibilities. Whenever it was his turn to serve on the construction site or in the kitchen, he moved into the onsite mobile homes, along with the building volunteers. A top executive in the organization would polish and waterproof stone while managing the organization's day-to-day activities. This balance of juggling various types of seva without bearing the burden of his position has inspired thousands of business owners, directors, and chief executives to follow in his footsteps and adopt the core lesson of Hinduism—they have looked past their identity and status, realized their atman, and turned to serve the Divine and its creation through the building of this Akshardham. Their stories of seva resonate with humility.

THE EYE DOCTOR WHO DID

Dr. Nikita Patel was pleasantly stunned after being asked to lead the team preparing and treating the stones before assembly, despite having only been at the Akshardham construction site for a few weeks. Nikita realized that this would be extremely different from her normal work, especially so because this was the first working environment where everyone wanted to be there to serve but wanted nothing in return. No one needed to be told to serve; they just needed to be guided, comforted, and encouraged.

A few weeks prior, Nikita and her husband had locked up their home in Cleveland, Ohio, and moved to New Jersey to serve full-time in the mandir construction project. She had recently completed her medical training and was working as an ophthalmologist. She did not know the first thing about coating stones with substances. Over time, Nikita became effective at using a forklift to lift stones and chemically treat them. At one point, she even learned how to fix broken machines and tools. Never in her life had she imagined that her trained hands would translate to construction site work.

It takes an extraordinary amount of courage and faith for both a young wife and husband to leave their professional jobs to come serve full-time in a different state. The logistics, financial planning, and anxiety were not easy to manage at first. However, her first day on "the seva" put her at ease. She not only learned how to be an effective leader, but she also continued her seva for the organization as a youth program coordinator. It was as if she was managing two full-time, equally important jobs, with an overarching sense of joy and satisfaction that she had never felt before.

Politeness and positivity became a staple in her tone. She gained the self-confidence to take on any task. When asked what she would urge visitors to look for when they visit Akshardham, she responded, "Listen for the stories of the bhaktas who loved and served without any desire for recognition or appreciation. No one wanted anything except to please their guru and to give back to the community. This spirit will truly change the way you see and experience the architecture and the energy of the space." Nikita and her husband served at Akshardham until the completion of the construction. These lessons will change her long after she moves back to Cleveland with her husband. This power couple was one of several to alter their lives willingly to contribute to Akshardham.

FROM 200 FEET ABOVE

For almost twelve years now, Sanjay Patel and a couple of his colleagues have operated cranes for the Akshardham construction. After learning that contracting for crane operators is one of the largest expenses for the community, the three of them decided to get licensed and certified by the state. They paid for the courses and exams and, in turn, donated the next decade of their lives to service at the Akshardham construction site. They first began operating smaller cranes for the construction of the shikharbaddha mandir and smaller buildings. When it was time to begin construction on the Mahamandir, they shifted to the tower crane, which stands 200 feet above the ground. It takes an experienced operator at least five minutes to climb a narrow channel of stairs up to the top.

Operating a crane requires patience and expertise. Rain or shine, they showed daily. A senior sadhu shared a valuable observation, "The stones and the volunteers all kept changing. These three were constant." Though all their stories are admirable, Sanjay's story stands out.

Sanjay has a medical condition that leads to frequent kidney stones. The pain is often unbearable, yet he has never missed a day of service. The sadhus and volunteers tried to convince him to change his seva for the project. He, however, was determined. He knew just how critical his skills were. At one point, his condition had so worsened that a special pin was put in his kidney to drain an infection. His fellow volunteers urged Sanjay to take a few weeks off from seva. He was undeterred. He would slowly climb up the crane and, after twenty minutes, finally reach his seat. His colleagues noticed the pain on his face, but his smile and commitment were equally present. Sanjay continued to serve throughout his two-week recovery period.

The ultimate test of his enthusiasm and dedication came on a day that started like any other. Sanjay served earlier that morning on the crane before heading home to pick up his father for a doctor's appointment. It was there, in his presence, that his father suffered a heart attack and passed away at 9 am. Sanjay attended to the immediate arrangements for his father. He showered and said his prayers in accordance with Hindu tradition. An hour after his father passed away, Sanjay was back on site, in his seat 200 feet in the sky. When asked why he did not take even that one day off from seva, Sanjay shared an inspiring perspective. "I have alerted my brothers, and we are arranging for our father's last rites. In the meantime, being here with my seva family makes me feel calm, reassured, and loved. What better way to honor my father than to serve in his memory."

For many others, just like Sanjay, they derive a sense of palpable fulfilment and centeredness from seva that helps them cope with anxiety, loss, and pain. For them, in seva is an antidote to dealing with life's difficulties.

A PARTNER IN SERVICE

Born and raised in an accepting and at once traditional Lebanon in the early 1960s, S. Maurice Rached was taught to experience the world with an open mind and learn from those who were different. This one foundational thought would shape his journey when he immigrated to New Jersey in the 1980s. In 2008, he would find a Hindu community that would share those values and accept him with open arms as a "bhakta"—a partner in service.

By the early 2000s, Maurice had established himself as one of the premier traffic and environmental engineers in the region. BAPS was just beginning its design for the Akshardham project. Maurice remembers how he felt in his first interaction with Hari Patel and other local volunteers. "I noticed three important values that made me want to be a part of the project. First, I was moved by the spirit of volunteerism in the community. Anyone would serve in any which way when called upon. It was truly humbling to see wealthy, educated, qualified professionals serving in ways that would seem beneath their pay grade in the real world. There was something spiritual about it. Second, I was moved by the way people gave financially. This project was not built using corporate donations or wealthy donors. Every single volunteer who contributed time also contributed an unimaginable amount of his or her own resources for the completion of the project. I was inspired to donate hours and hours of my time through their spirit of giving. Finally, I cannot satisfactorily explain this last emotion. But when I walk on to this campus, I feel a sense of peace and calm. Many people attribute it to that feeling they get when participating in the rituals inside the temple. For me, it is a feeling that I have had since the first day I set foot on this parcel of land. There is an inherent sense of tranquility that keeps drawing me back to this project and the community. For me, this project is not a task or a client. It is my seva."

Maurice now regularly visits the mandir with his family. The first time his brother returned from Lebanon after recovering from his injuries in the 2020 Beirut port explosion, Maurice brought him to the mandir to receive blessings and to meet his seva family.

The sense of warmth and openness that Maurice experienced on the site is reflective of the community's ethos. Anyone willing to serve and love based on these principles, regardless of their background, feels at home at Akshardham.

BRIDGING THE GAP: SADHUS IN SEVA

In Hindu communities, sadhus or swamis hold a special place of reverence, not because they are seen as more important hierarchically, but because of what they symbolize and who they represent. In the Swaminarayan tradition, sadhus follow eight-fold celibacy and detachment from their birth families. They do not speak to members of the opposite gender as a part of their spiritual vows of celibacy, except in case of a life-threatening emergency. On your visit to Akshardham, you may see sadhus serving or interacting with visitors. When approached by a female visitor, the sadhus will respectfully walk or turn away. This gesture is not to insult or offend women, but rather to preserve the sanctity of their own vow of detachment. They also refrain from keeping monetary possessions. Sadhus are permitted to use technology and convenience products needed to assist in their day-to-day seva for coordination, counseling, and communication. And yet, they are urged to center themselves in a way that is indicative of the true yogi—amid society, loving and serving alongside others without attachment to their tasks, without expectations for praise, and without power.

Despite such austere vows and guidelines, these sadhus play a critical role in the integration of the different communities at Akshardham, as well as a bridge between generations. Prashantdarshandas Swami has been involved in the building of mandirs since he was initiated as a sadhu in saffron garb. He also served during the recovery and rebuilding effort following the Gujarat Earthquake of 2001.

Drawing inspiration from the other full-time volunteers at Akshardham who worked tirelessly while putting aside their station in society, Prashantdarshandas Swami chose to serve as a facilitator and sevak. **He helped create a seva family between people of different economic and linguistic** backgrounds. He also paid attention to the needs of the volunteers. He celebrated Holi (the festival of colors) and other festivals with them. He made special arrangements for some of them to perform rituals for the deity of architecture, Vishvakarma. He remembered their birthdays. He served and fed the volunteers, including the skilled artisan volunteers, often with his own hands. Feeding someone with your own hands is a sign of love and blessing in the Hindu tradition.

Most importantly, Prashantdarshandas Swami realized that though the skilled artisan volunteers were serving here, they had left a part of their hearts in India with their wives and families. He made it a point to care for their families in India. He would encourage devotees to assist with medical emergencies and school tuition for the volunteers' children. In one unique instance, he even arranged for two volunteers and sadhus from the community in Jaipur to go to a hospital and donate blood to save the nephew of a skilled artisan volunteer serving in Robbinsville. That blood donation in the middle of the night helped save the life of that young man. This level of commitment and care set a standard for all those around him. The other sadhus and American volunteers also bonded with the skilled artisan volunteers. They ate scrumptious meals together, played cricket and volleyball, and sang and danced to bhakti melodies together.

Over time, fifty more sadhus and sadhus-in training joined the project. Though many of them had served in the construction of a mandir in Sarangpur, India, and refined these skills through special mandir-building courses, Prashantdarshandas Swami helped them acclimate to the ongoing project. He led by example. He could be seen walking around the site picking up trash or serving food to the volunteers. The young sadhus learned that their mentor was not just a master builder, but a master sevak.

Prashantdarshandas Swami also designed a novel way to assemble entire portions of the steeples and ornate stone ceilings on the ground before being raised by the cranes to be placed on the structure. This had never been done in the building of mandirs in India. Scholars of ancient Hindu architecture verified that this was never mentioned in theory in past texts either. Maximizing the use of volunteers on the ground allowed for the assembly teams to move efficiently, safely, and without interference at higher altitudes. The women volunteers who oversaw the assembling of the stone structures on the ground were able to create with perfection. Though this innovation is now being used and discussed all over mandir sites in India, Prashantdarshandas Swami refuses to take credit. "I do not quite remember who thought of this idea. I am sure it was one of the younger sadhus or senior volunteers." His expertise came only second to his ability to empower others.

Though traditional skill and innovation were instrumental in completing this project, it is not merely this knowhow or expertise that deserve credit. The latter phase of this project was accomplished by the coming together of sadhus and community volunteers who were guided and trained by skilled volunteers. It is the organization's environment of inclusivity, unity, personal and spiritual growth, enthusiasm, and faith-based dedication that allowed for these results.

* * *

This is just a refrain from the song of each bhakta and sadhu. There are so many more verses and songs. It is impossible to list them all, but it is important to acknowledge the contributions of volunteers who served crucial, long-term functions in the building of Akshardham, even if only in silence…

WHERE SMILES BUILD BRIDGES

An additional 12,491 other volunteers who have contributed to Akshardham through bhakti and seva remain unnamed, and their stories unheard and unshared for now. This is perhaps so that they can be witnessed and experienced firsthand in Robbinsville, New Jersey. Seva with inclusiveness, enthusiasm, and self-development gives way to the smiles one sees at Akshardham. These genuine smiles build bridges between communities that may have otherwise feared or distrusted each other. The next song is of the collaboration and cooperation between BAPS and a small town that changed New Jersey's landscape forever. The stones sing of Robbinsville, Akshardham's forever home.

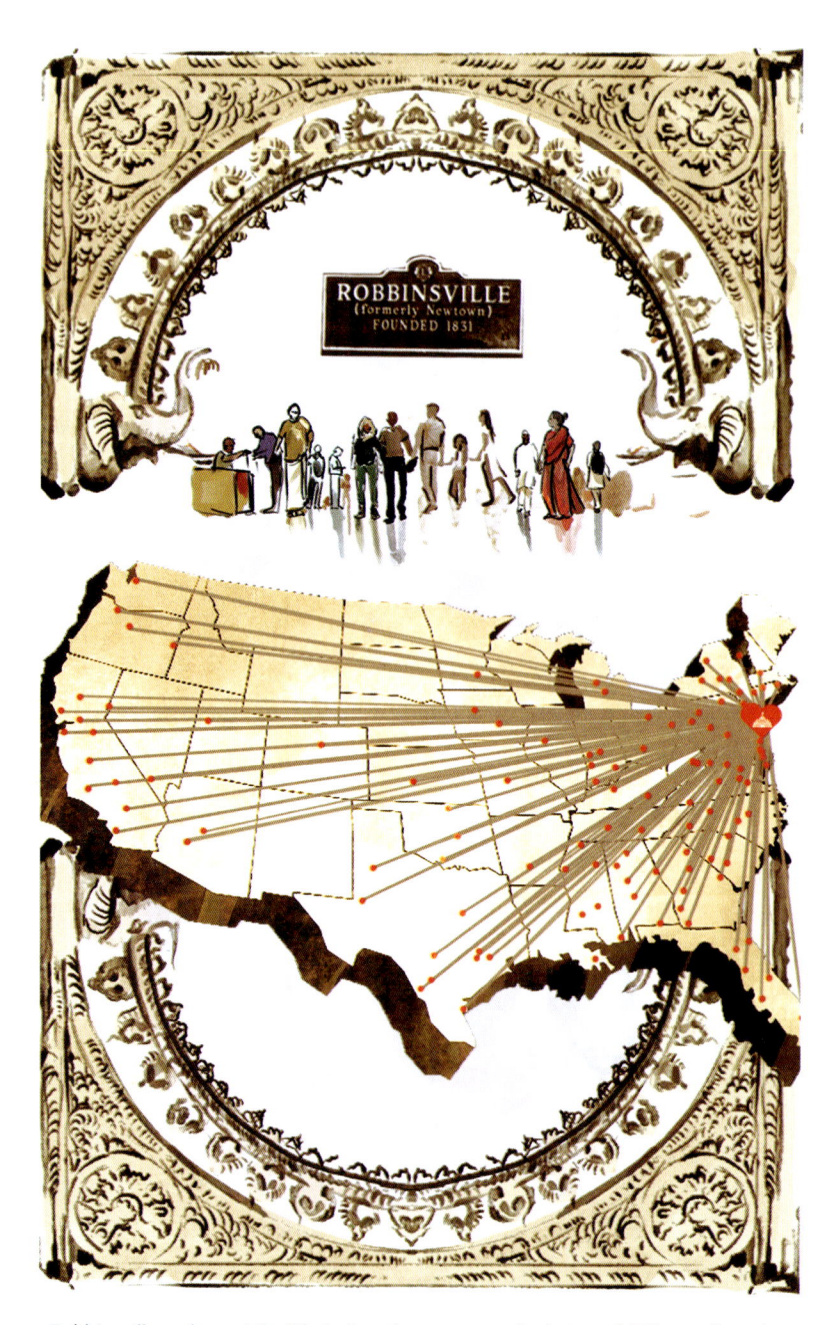

Robbinsville embraced the Hindu American community. In turn, BAPS contributed to its social, spiritual, humanitarian, and architectural landscape. Diverse visitors and volunteers from around the nation were drawn to Akshardham over the last decade. A new Robbinsivlle-BAPS family came to be. Robbinsville became the center of it all!

5

The Song of Robbinsville, New Jersey: A Forever Home

―――◆◆◆―――

WHAT STARTED ON A PAPER NAPKIN…

Ancient Indian stories of wisdom and auspicious beginnings often start with a gathering of people sitting under the shade of a tree. The story of Akshardham in Robbinsville can be traced back to a similar informal interaction under a tree on a soy farm in 2008. A group of senior sadhus who had been responsible for the design of the Akshardham complexes in New Delhi and Gandhinagar and other marvelous BAPS mandirs visited the 102-acre soy farm in Robbinsville Township for the first time. During the thirty-minute ride from the BAPS mandir in Edison, the team discussed how the land should ideally be serene, spacious, and secluded, while also amidst a vibrant and accepting community.

Hindu mandirs in America have a long history of facing tough inquiries from local town development boards who are unfamiliar with the sights, sounds, and scents of the community. In the past, BAPS North America has done a great job presenting their project plans in communities across the country. Many localities who were hesitant to back an unfamiliar religious community and its customs came to understand and eventually supported the project with enthusiasm. BAPS Shri Swaminarayan Mandir in Chino Hills, California, is a prime example of how neighbors and BAPS partnered together to educate and accommodate each other.

The community leaders knew that it was not enough to select a parcel of land merely based on convenience and design compatibility. Warmth, acceptance, and fair-mindedness were just as, if not more, vital. What follows is the stones' song of how BAPS and the Robbinsville community collaborated—how they formed a Robbinsville-BAPS family.

As the sadhus surveyed the plot of land, Ishwarcharandas Swami could not contain his excitement, and it spilled over onto his face. It was love at first sight. He just knew that Pramukh Swami Maharaj would love this property. He asked for a piece of paper and pencil. A scrap piece of paper and a paper napkin were the best the group could muster up. Shreejiswarupdas Swami, Aksharvatsaldas Swami, and Bhaktinandandas Swami started to sketch according to the senior sadhu's guidance. In a matter of minutes, the team penned the rough layout of Akshardham. The project masterplan today resembles that first sketch. When asked, each of the members sing the same tune. "The initial design was nothing but divine intervention and inspiration. How else could we have sketched a plan that would be the standing blueprint almost a decade and a half later?"

On a recent visit to the mandir, Mayor David Fried let the sadhus and BAPS leadership in on a secret, "You ended up making an extensive presentation on the project and the masterplan a few months later. But my team and I were sold on your commitment to serve and share positivity. We would have said "yes" even if you brought us that sketch on a paper napkin! Some things are predetermined. With hard work and pure intent everything falls into place." This sort of enthusiasm and support were shown by many members of the town council and planning board. Many of them were excited that the community would receive something beyond a commercial or manufacturing facility. A landmark for faith, culture, and architecture would mean that there would be an addition to the social and spiritual landscape of the blossoming community.

After exploring 246 possible sites over a decade and purchasing two others, BAPS selected Robbinsville. And Robbinsville selected BAPS. Like the motto of the township says, Robbinsville became "the center of it all" for Hindus and Indians for generations to come.

Although Pramukh Swami Maharaj did not visit Robbinsville until 2014, he offered five key points of guidance and blessing for finding a home for Akshardham in America. First, the parcel of land should be at least 100 acres large. This would allow for ample space to build the complex and leave enough land for conservation and environmental initiatives.

Second, the land should be favorably zoned for principal use as a house of worship. Re-zoning a piece of land, especially for a large Hindu mandir, would be an uphill battle. Third, the plot for the project should be within 108 miles of the first BAPS Shri Swaminarayan Mandir in North America in Flushing, Queens, New York. This would ensure its proximity to New York City, an advanced, large metropolitan city, as well as the community's humble roots. Fourth, the land should be accessible by a major highway and a series of major roads. NJ Turnpike (Interstate 95) was a highway that Pramukh Swami Maharaj was well acquainted with—he had spent many a night visiting the homes of bhaktas and attending assemblies in various towns and cities along that highway. He knew that the major roadway was a lifeline that connected the region and the nation. In a meeting with senior devotees, he ran his finger across the map over the NJ Turnpike and insisted on trying to locate Akshardham near it.

Finally, Pramukh Swami Maharaj knew that one can build a home only where one is wanted and accepted. The local leaders would have to celebrate the project's wins and stand shoulder to shoulder with the Hindu community when difficulties arose. Over the years it has become clear to all who visit that Robbinsville is the ideal community where the guru's five requirements are met. Robbinsville Township is not just a location; it is a forever home for Akshardham. This project was crucial not only for BAPS but also for the growing number of Indian families and businesses in the neighborhood.

INDIANS IN ROBBINSVILLE

Robbinsville, and Central New Jersey in general, boasts a diverse population. Of the approximately 3 million Hindus in North America, more than 35 percent reside in New York, New Jersey, Connecticut, and Pennsylvania. Indian migration to New York City, North New Jersey, and Philadelphia eventually spilt into the quaint towns of Central and South Jersey. Today, nearly 30% of Robbinsville's population is of Indian heritage. Neighboring towns in Central Jersey also proudly celebrate their diversity with populations from South Asia, East Asia, Eastern Europe, and the Middle East. This diversity and the heavy concentration of Hindus and Indians in the regional community is another reason that Akshardham was built in Robbinsville. With such a large community of bhaktas in the region, it was only natural to select a plot of land nearly equidistant from Philadelphia and New York City, as well as from Washington D.C. and Boston.

The Indian American community beyond BAPS is also active in Robbinsville and Central Jersey. Indians from Gujarat, Rajasthan, Tamil Nadu, Andhra Pradesh, Punjab, Maharashtra, and Bengal are part of the community's social fabric. There are several houses of worship, including a beautiful Sikh Gurudwara that visitors will see on the right side of the road before entering Akshardham. Cultural programs such as Holi and Diwali celebrations, along with regular home *satsang* (spiritual congregation) activities by various Hindu, Jain, and Sikh communities, keep the community connected. Finally, Robbinsville and the neighboring towns are proud of their

Robbinsville Premier Cricket League, India's favorite pastime. Local cultural centers, house of worship, and businesses often support these cricket clubs and the role they play in uniting Indian Americans with the rest of the community through sport.

Living in Robbinsville has its advantages, and that is why so many Indian Americans and diverse communities have settled in its vicinity. According to a recent article on TAPinto.net, Robbinsville is currently the second-best place to buy a home and raise a family in New Jersey. The crime rates are low, it is affordable, and the school district encourages children to achieve balanced growth and stability. The township and its neighboring communities are also celebrated for having accessible administrations that reason and work for their residents.

The bustling energy and growth of the township has benefitted dearly from the presence of these immigrant communities. Their presence have made contributions to the development of residential properties, professional services, small businesses and, most importantly, the cultural vibrance that builds bridges between many groups and their complexities. The most tangible sensory and spiritual experience of India in the area, however, is brought on by the presence of Akshardham.

BAPS IN THE LOCAL COMMUNITY

Several leaders over two generations from BAPS North America remember a variation of this conversation with Pramukh Swami Maharaj. Since his first visit to America in 1974, the guru's primary guidelines about building mandirs had nothing to do with selecting the correct stone or an appropriate plot of land. The first rule was always concerning being a good neighbor, a good community member. Pramukh Swami Maharaj used to say, "Remember, we are moving into their home. Our bhaktas and visitors should be mindful not only of local laws and regulations, but also customs, traditions, and preferences. Participate in local events and stand by the community during their difficulties. Give from the little we have. We are a part of their family. Be a responsible *nagrik* (citizen). Respect people and their ways, and they will welcome us."

This mantra was the key to the exponential growth of BAPS in North America. In less than five decades, the community went from having one mandir in a small basement in Flushing, New York, to building more than 100 mandirs in America as well as Akshardham in Robbinsville. Each of these mandirs rest upon the organization's sincere efforts to fit into the social fabric of each local community.

In Robbinsville, BAPS made the effort to build bridges with neighboring residents and business owners as well. One of the closest neighbors is Tony's Farm and Garden Center, across the road on Route 130. Chris Ciaccio has been a curious mind and supporter of BAPS since the inception of the project. Reaching out to her has resulted in her reaching out to others. Ravi Patni, a member of the local BAPS community and a Robbinsville resident, recalls one such visit to the local nursery with his daughters to purchase shrubs and plants for his backyard. She creates opportunities for Ravi and others to share their story. "Have you been to BAPS? Ravi volunteers there. You should go check out the temple. It is beautiful and they do great work in the community. Ravi, tell Sarah more about the mandir and the work you do…"

One of the concerns of the local community was the change the mandir's steeples would make to the historic viewshed. When driving down over the hill from West Windsor, one is transported back to a town from 200 years ago. Add a large Hindu mandir with grand steeples to that view and the change in look and feel of the colonial town with farms and fields would be noticeable, if not overpowering. BAPS proactively addressed the residents' trepidations by suggesting a creative solution. They flew a bright red blimp through the fields where the tallest steeples of the mandir would be erected. They then modified the plans so that the Mahamandir views would not grossly impede the line of sight. The intention was to respect the past that the local community so cherished. There was a way to adapt and preserve tradition, and BAPS was able to find a solution with the help of the township's leadership and several imaginative consultants.

BAPS also joins in and serves at local events and parades. The St. Patrick's Day Parade, Community Day Celebrations, National Night Out, and the 150th birthday of the township are just a few of the events in which BAPS has actively participated and contributed through its volunteers. Imagine a Hindu mandir being the grand marshal at a parade organized by the local Irish community. Mayor Fried was quoted as saying, "Only in Robbinsville can that happen." The late Dave Doran, vice president of the parade, explained why BAPS worked as a celebrated partner. "The reason we chose BAPS is because they have significant impact on the culture and lifestyle of our community. They have embraced service to others, which is a tenet important to us as members of the Robbinsville Irish Heritage Association. We have more in common than most realize."

BAPS never misses an opportunity to serve at township humanitarian events. Mayor Fried remembers an instance when he called the leadership at BAPS Robbinsville to help with a township-organized blood donation drive in the aftermath of a devastating fire in nearby Ewing Township. A simple call to serve is all it took the bhaktas from Robbinsville and the neighboring townships to queue up to donate blood in a matter of hours. The turnout was so overwhelming that the township called BAPS at 6 p.m. to not send any more bhaktas! Similar ongoing donations are made to the Robbinsville Food Pantry, the local Fire and Police Departments, and local schools, including the high school's robotics club and athletic fields. During COVID, BAPS volunteers regularly delivered care packages and PPE material. Bhakti and seva, again, were the driving forces for serving and loving the local community in Robbinsville and the neighboring towns in Mercer County.

THE ROBBINSVILLE COMMUNITY AT BAPS AKSHARDHAM

Understanding communities of faith is key to overcoming fear of the unknown. Akshardham always opens its doors to the community. From Open House events to individual invitations for neighbors and residents, the community seeks to create a welcoming and accessible environment, even for those unfamiliar with Hindu customs and traditions. Bhaktas prepare special introductions and programs to integrate the first-time visitor into the Hindu community. Akshardham is certainly a Hindu place of worship, but also a home for the broader community.

A prominent example of this was when BAPS Robbinsville turned its gymnasium and assembly hall into an emergency shelter for local community members during Hurricane Sandy in 2012. Hours after the county and township made calls to BAPS leadership about housing people who had been displaced from the mobile home park, BAPS set up a temporary shelter with warm meals and beverages, as well as welcoming smiles. They also housed a group of one hundred truckers who had driven from Louisiana with fuel for local emergency facilities. The space was more than a shelter. It became a home that invited all those who needed warmth and comfort during that difficult time.

Residents and community leaders treat Akshardham like their own. Bhaktas often notice Robbinsville residents bringing guests or family members on a visit to the mandir. The enthusiasm and aptitude with which they give tours rival the guides from within the BAPS community. They do not have a script. They witnessed and watched the mandir come up. They are "bhaktas" in that they believed in the power of bhakti and seva—the spirit of BAPS. They are not showing a mandir to someone. They are showing "their" mandir to their loved ones.

VOICES OF SUPPORT FROM THE LOCAL COMMUNITY

Just as it was impossible to include the stories of all those who served to build the mandir, it is impossible to include stories of all the neighbors and community leaders who have voiced their support over the last decade and a half. These voices are of people who do not attend BAPS spiritual assemblies or even live a Hindu lifestyle, but who looked after the project. They guided and even cautioned—whatever it took to get things done right. They were, in essence, a bridge between ancient India and modern Robbinsville. The scope and scale of the project was unlike anything Robbinsville had ever experienced. They were determined to create history. For them, BAPS' success story was Robbinsville's success story. Most importantly, they stood by the community through its high and low moments. This loyalty was rooted in the conviction of their shared experiences of the BAPS-Robbinsville family. In their own way, they too loved and served, participating in bhakti and seva as "bhaktas."

Mayor Dave Fried is one of the first and most consistent voices of support and guidance. His ability to draw together members of the community and help BAPS translate its ideas in a way that is accessible to those who have never worked with a Hindu or faith-based community is priceless. Cultural translation is a special skill that the mayor has mastered. He stood with BAPS. But he also never shied away from giving clear advice on how to better execute or prepare for events and interactions with the community. The town's business administrator, **Joy Tozzi**, showed similar support through innovative guidance. Though they did not offer any favors, they were keen to help the two communities understand each other—to become one family.

Jerry Dasti, the attorney for the Robbinsville Township

Planning Board, balanced the community's religious freedoms to build a house of worship according to the ancient Hindu architectural tradition, while also considering local guidelines and concerns. Over time, he too became a part of the BAPS-Robbinsville family and attended key milestones with his family.

Vince Calcagno, Chris Ciaccio, and Ron Witt and various members of the Town Council represent the Robbinsville spirit of acceptance and inclusivity. The council had the foresight to see the growth and development the influx of believers and visitors would bring to the township. They did what was in the best interests of the township while believing in the spirit of the project. They knew that the project would add to the various landscapes of the township for generations to come.

Frank Cettina, Daniel Jackson, and Sheree McGowan and other members of the Planning and Zoning Board served Robbinsville and BAPS with their diligence. After presiding over the first meeting pertaining to BAPS' application for the mandir in 2008, many of them appreciated the thoroughness and directness in the presentation. After becoming intimately familiar with the community's religious beliefs and architectural tradition, they were pleased to preside over the subsequent four applications. All the applications were approved without having to compromise any of the township's concerns or guidelines.

Tim McGough was one of the first "bridge builders" between BAPS and the local community. Early on, Tim was the Township Engineer and Business Administrator. His technical expertise was critical to BAPS being able to adapt traditional

Hindu architecture with the requirements and sensitivities of the township. His personal statements on BAPS and technical testimony during the public hearings for Akshardham illustrate his passion for BAPS' modus operandi—selfless service and love.

Hal English is the President of the Princeton Chamber of Commerce and the former Community Development Director of Robbinsville Township. He seamlessly took over Tim's role and helped BAPS explain the technical aspects of their plans to the community. A strong proponent of bringing people to the mandir, he knows that no presentation, phone call, or publication can do justice to the story the stones sing. Hal often remembers the spirit of service and volunteerism at BAPS when addressing other non-profits. "I work with volunteers on my committee, but here [at BAPS] these volunteers are perfect. The 600-plus volunteers who have served here are perfect. The work that they are doing is absolutely perfect because their heart is in it. The love. They are making sure they are doing it with their all. It is such a calling. Such an honor. Just as it has been for me."

Ann Bell, John Nunziato, and Paul Renaud were crucial in their role as facilitators and area experts. As staff members for the township and the Buildings Department, they were responsible for seeing the project to completion. During the early stages, there was a real sense of "unknown" around the Akshardham Mahamandir. They took the time out to learn about Indian stone architecture. Their diligent efforts ensured that the community built a house of worship that complied with both the township's regulations and ancient sacred texts.

The neighbors in town were equally welcoming. **Matthew and Kurt Gabart** grew up a few blocks from where Akshardham sits. Their childhood dirt bike paths had now been transformed into a house of worship. One afternoon, sadhus from the mandir crossed over to the brothers' property. Matthew did not stop them but started a conversation about plants, nurseries, and farming. It was the start of a friendship. The Gabart brothers shared their knowledge of agriculture with BAPS volunteers, and even volunteered their time and farming equipment to help the volunteers prepare the lush gardens for Akshardham. Dozens of other neighbors also enjoy serving and learning as part of the Robbinsville-BAPS family.

Amit Chopra, Priya Kushnoor Viswanathan, Umang Naik, Jai Gulati and several others along with their families from the Indian American community in Robbinsville accept and celebrate the mandir as their own. As shared in the second chapter, India and Hinduism are extremely diverse, yet in Robbinsville they have all come together as vocal proponents of Akshardham. They educate other Indians and members of the Robbinsville community about Akshardham. Amit, and others like him, have expressed, "This mandir is a source of pride for all Hindus and Indians. Our children will grow up asking about our heritage and tradition. We do not have to fly all the way back to India to show them. We have a piece of it right here in our backyards."

The community's first line of heroes, **the Police, Fire, EMS, and Public Works** have truly supported the making of Akshardham by providing their service in the case of emergencies or the gathering of large crowds. Emergency Services always rushed in case a volunteer or visitor was injured. The police and other facilitators were always available early in the morning and late into the night to help BAPS navigate and direct traffic during large festivals and when the guru visited in 2014, 2017, and 2023. These first responders and facilitators have always shown professionalism and generosity as bhaktas of the community while serving alongside BAPS volunteers. Do not be surprised if you see Sergeant Scott Kivet and his team directing traffic and greeting visitors with their hands folded in the traditional Hindu greeting!

WHAT IS POSSIBLE WHEN YOU LOVE, SERVE, AND EMBRACE…

Through open rapport and by finding acceptance in Robbinsville to build Akshardham, Hindus from all over the region and country have found a forever home. They are indebted to the hundreds of Robbinsville residents who made this possible. **Akshardham stands as a testament that diverse communities can fuse into a single family.** The township has always tried to find a way to make things work. And that is what family does. **Thomas Halm**, a Robbinsville resident and attorney, said it best in an interview with Michele Alperin, "Robbinsville found a good partner in BAPS because they were anxious to do something interesting, to be a good neighbor. BAPS found a good partner in somebody who was not afraid of something different and to learn from others." Robbinsville is a forever home for Hindus in America, and Akshardham is a home for the local community. For BAPS, this song, and all the songs before it, have been lived by the inspirers of Akshardham: the gurus.

Pramukh Swami Maharaj and Mahant Swami Maharaj are pictured here with their creation, BAPS Swaminarayan Akshardham, Robbinsville, New Jersey. Akshardham's inception, creation, and completion are examples of the gurus' constant, humanly divine presence in a spiritual aspirant's life.

6

The Song of the Inspirers: Gurus as Exemplars of Bhakti and Seva

―――◆―――

THE GURU IN THE SWAMINARAYAN HINDU TRADITION

A five-year-old child stole away from his mother to run to the stage where the guru was delivering his katha to hundreds. He had waddled his way up the steps before she could get someone to grab him. The guru watched the child approach him. The child's smile mirrored that of the guru's. At that moment, the entire assembly could feel their guru's gaze on them. The guru called the child closer and asked him to bow to the murti of Bhagwan Swaminarayan to his right. The boy instead rushed to touch his guru's feet. As the child darted off the stage, an onlooker asked him why he did not bow to the murti first. The innocent boy sheepishly smiled and explained, "Well, the guru smiles at me and blesses me. Isn't the murti speaking through him?" The boy had probably never sung the devotional couplet by the renowned bhakti poet Kabir, "If guru and God appeared in front of me, to whom shall I bow first? I submit to the guru, for he is the one who journeys [with] me to the Divine," but his response perfectly captured its sentiment. He just wanted to feel warmth, attention, and comfort. This spiritual intimacy is the hallmark of the guru and bhakta relationship.

Gurus are not only teachers, guides, inspirers, and exemplars; they are walking partners on the journey we call life and, for many Hindus, the journey we call *lives*. They live and love in a way that creates an environment of growth and integration. Their lives teach one the balance of succeeding with stability. They set an example of love and service that inspires one to be a better person—a better parent, better child, better sibling, better builder, better professor, better author, better reader, better chef, better entrepreneur, better healthcare professional, and even better patient. You get the point. Gurus also spread this song of selfless love, service, and inclusivity to anyone willing to listen and learn.

Pramukh Swami Maharaj (1921–2016) and his successor Mahant Swami Maharaj (born 1933) have led the current generation in the BAPS community as exemplars of bhakti and seva. Gurus within the community are often referred to as 'Swamishri'. Simply put, Akshardham would not have been created or completed if it were not for the gurus. Pramukh Swami Maharaj created an environment of bhakti, seva, and inclusivity through his interactions. He was the inspirer who blessed the community to purchase the land, design the master plans, receive approval from the township, and commence construction. Mahant Swami Maharaj played a crucial role in inspiring the bhaktas to complete Akshardham after his guru's passing away. When the community faced difficulty, his unwavering faith in the Divine and the community inspired thousands to serve until the completion of this landmark, and to do so with a smile and without malice. This is the story of the gurus' bhakti and seva—the bhakti and seva they inspired in thousands. It is the crescendo among all the songs the stones sing at Akshardham.

PRAMUKH SWAMI MAHARAJ: EMPOWERING THROUGH FAITH AND LEADERSHIP

Pramukh Swami Maharaj was the fifth, and arguably the most well-known, spiritual successor of Bhagwan Swaminarayan. His simplicity and humility touched the hearts of millions. At the same time, his effectiveness as a humanitarian, social integrator, and cultural ambassador generated a social and spiritual renaissance that resonated with people from all backgrounds. **He set an example for how a Swaminarayan Hindu should practice their faith while embracing those of others.** He built bridges between his community and that of others by reaching out to Hindu, Jain, Sikh, Jewish, Muslim, and Christian leaders from across the world. His famed conversation with Pope John Paul II in Vatican City in 1984 and his address to the United Nations Millenium World Peace Summit in 2000, urging respect and dialogue between religious leaders to create an environment of acceptance among followers are hallmarks of his all-embracing persona. Other religious leaders, heads of state, and marginalized members of society praise his work to reform social hierarchies through equality and inclusivity. He inspired over 1,200 Hindu mandirs and two Akshardham complexes in New Delhi and Gandhinagar, and he initiated more than 1,000 sadhus into the saffron garb. The mandirs became centers for cultural transmission and spiritual growth, while the sadhus followed in his footsteps as social reformers, spiritual counselors, and keepers of faith and tradition. More about his life can be learned from two recent publications. *In Love, At Ease: Everyday Spirituality with Pramukh Swami* (Penguin, 2023) weaves together the stories of hundreds from across the world to describe the guru, in the voice of a young scholar, journalist, and bhakta who grew up in the guru's presence. *Transcendence: My Spiritual Experiences with Pramukh Swamiji* (Harper Collins, 2016) captures the spiritual and professional journey of former President of India, Dr. A.P.J. Abdul Kalam, enriched by the guru.

On 8 December 1997, Swamishri was in Atladra (Vadodara), Gujarat. One of the senior sadhus in the community had just returned from a three-month tour of North America. Swayamprakashdas Swami (Doctor Swami) bowed to Swamishri. He shared his observations from his travels. "Swamishri, the satsang community is developing swiftly. I know you have willed to build several traditional stone mandirs and an Akshardham in America. Based on my experience, New Jersey would be the ideal place for Akshardham. The community is vibrant. It is close to major cities and the majority of the Indian American community…" Before he could complete his sentence, the guru interjected, "Doctor Swami, I agree. Akshardham must be built in New Jersey. Future generations will stay connected to their past and find spiritual solace through Akshardham. I am confident that the bhaktas and the community will come together to build it." Since that evening in 1997, Swamishri expressed his wish to build Akshardham on more than a dozen occasions.

He articulated this wish in different ways. At times, he professed a *sankalp* (formal ritual wish of conviction and dedication). On other occasions, Swamishri offered prayers and joined in the singing of *dhun* (chanting a mantra as a prayer) to complete that sankalp. He also wrote his blessings on maps, blueprints, and in the journals of senior bhaktas and sadhus. The end outcome of the sankalp and prayers was a collective commitment of all the bhaktas who heard and read their guru's words. They knew fulfilling their guru's wish to build Akshardham was their most direct and immediate bhakti and seva to Bhagwan Swaminarayan, their guru, and the community.

Swamishri's firm resolve was rooted in his strong faith in the Divine and his bhaktas. Kanu Patel recalls a meeting with the guru when the community was preparing a presentation of the master plan. Most of the collected funds had already been used to purchase the plot of land and prepare it for construction. The guru was in Gondal, India, on a cool October night in 2009. Kanu Patel expressed his reservations about the scale of the project. "Swamishri, we are almost out of funds, and we are only just getting ready to start construction. I am worried. What, how, who, when…"

Swamishri eased his trepidations. "Kanu, faith is the pillar of success and achievement. Are you building this for yourself or me? We are building it as a sign of our devotion to Bhagwan Swaminarayan. We are building it to give back to our community and future generations of Hindus and Indians in America. Have faith and instruct others to do the same. Bhagwan Swaminarayan will complete this project for us. None of us are doing it alone. God creates through his bhaktas. Why have you lost faith in the community? They gave their all for this project even before we settled on a plot of land. They will give until the Mahamandir is inaugurated. No matter how long it takes. I have complete faith in their seva. Have a little faith in *my* bhaktas…" The volunteer executive realized that he was part of something much bigger, a project being offered at the feet of the Divine. **He just needed to serve with faith. God, guru, and the community would take care of the rest.**

Large projects that extend over such a long period of time can suffer without direction and inspiration. Pramukh Swami Maharaj guided and blessed during pivotal moments of the project. The guru was available at all hours of the day to comfort and guide, and he did so calmly. He did not take on the burden of decision-making. He would pray to the Divine before sharing a suggestion and then would rest the outcome at God's feet. This method eased the weight of the tasks and enabled local leaders to make decisions with clarity and confidence.

First, the guru was very clear on where to build. Finding a large plot of land in a welcoming community in the Northeast is a challenging task at best. While the land search team often lost hope and started looking for land all over the region, Swamishri was clear. He guided them back to Central New Jersey by the NJ Turnpike. Second, Swamishri encouraged the community to purchase land before beginning the approval process. This led the community to invest in three different plots of land. In the long run, this helped accelerate the building process. It also meant that the community could sell one of its previous land plots and apply those funds towards the mandir construction efforts.

Third, a great leader always knows when to move on. After the community faced some resistance in a nearby town, Swamishri blessed the leadership in America to look ahead. There was no reason to appeal, file a lawsuit, or lament via public debate. He knew an open-minded community would welcome such a well-intentioned project. This timely advice helped gear resources and efforts in Robbinsville without looking back at the past. **Fourth, an effective leader methodically scales up and does so patiently.** Instead of pushing to build the entire complex at once, Swamishri advised the leadership to develop the plans in phases. This gave hope to the community and comforted the township. After the smaller shikharbaddha mandir was completed without incident, the township gained confidence in the traditional building techniques essential for the Mahamandir. Over time, the BAPS community acquired adjacent pieces of land and developed the project in pursuit of their genuine goal to serve the Divine, their guru, and the community.

Fifth, the guru guided the leadership to embrace modern technology and innovation without sacrificing tradition and the scriptural processes to build such stone mandirs. As stated in Chapter 1, building stone mandirs in India is a nuanced, sacred process. Sacred architectural treatises have detailed drawings and instructions on building mandirs. Swamishri instructed Aksharvatsaldas Swami, Shreejiswarupdas Swami, Bhaktinandandas Swami, and Harshadbhai Chavda to listen to the Sompuras (traditional architects) and study the ancient texts before designing the ritual shikharbaddha mandir and the Mahamandir. "Aksharvatsaldas, I want you to research these texts before you start. Innovate with technology, but do not wander from our roots. Mandirs are the keepers of tradition. Follow the texts and ask experts." This became the framework from which the team advanced the design technologically, by using cutting-edge lighting and safety measures, while also maintaining traditional modes of Nagara-style mandir architecture. It is important to note that neither of the mandirs in Robbinsville have *ghummats* (arched domes). Instead, the sadhus and designers decided to revert to an earlier form of architecture with samarans and shikhars. As a result of the guru's encouragement and foresight, the team was able to successfully execute this mass exercise in the coming together of innovation and tradition at Akshardham.

Finally, Swamishri was never willing to take credit and deferred any praise. He always reminded the sadhus and bhaktas that it was all God's doing and that they were all just there to serve. By setting this example service without a focus on oneself, Swamishri inspired the community to serve and love without expecting and craving appreciation. It also fostered an environment of collaboration and cooperation over competition.

Swamishri wanted less for him, and more for the Divine and the community. He knew that bhaktas wanted to offer him the best of things as a sign of bhakti, but he led with modesty. During a meeting in the village of Limbdi in May 2011, and later again in a meeting in Sarangpur, Swamishri reviewed the Akshardham complex plans. Someone pointed to an area behind the mandir and referred to it as the 'guru's lodging'. Swamishri used that as a teaching moment. "I do not need a special residence. I am always on the move. Make it available to all senior sadhus. What is mine is all of yours. And keep it simple. Accommodation is meant for rest and work, not for extravagant displays. Use those resources to build the mandir or the classrooms for children's activities. No wood carvings. Is that clear?" The guru's ability to guide without carrying the weight of ownership allowed him to be the most effective member of the team. The rest of the bhaktas and sadhus followed in his steps.

In 2014, at the age of 92, Swamishri visited Robbinsville for the murti-pratishtha and inaugurated the ritual shikharbaddha mandir. He also performed the groundbreaking ceremony for the construction of the Mahamandir. It was to be his last trip to America. In 2016, Mahant Swami Maharaj assumed responsibilities of the community as guru and creator of Akshardham at the age of 82.

MAHANT SWAMI MAHARAJ: AN OFFERING TO HIS GURU

Mahant Swami Maharaj (Keshavjivandas Swami) was born on 13 September 1933. He was initiated into the sadhu-fold in 1957 by Pramukh Swami Maharaj's guru, Yogiji Maharaj. Before being initiated, he received a bachelor's degree in agriculture from Anand,

Gujarat. Even from his early days as a sadhu, he was seen as the wise and silent one who led by example. He traveled the globe upon his gurus' instructions and provided spiritual counseling and direction to bhaktas and sadhus. His silent presence and bold eyes inspired millions to find solace in faith and spirituality over the materialistic bustle of everyday life. After succeeding Pramukh Swami Maharaj as BAPS' spiritual guru and president, he immediately turned his attention to Akshardham in Robbinsville. He visited America in 2017 and assessed the progress of Akshardham. He followed up with sadhus regarding the design and carving of the stone. Senior sadhus recall one such conversation with the guru about the need for progress, without hampering quality. "Look, we want to get it done soon and done right. It must be perfect. It was Pramukh Swami Maharaj's wish to gift this to the community in America." Mahant Swami Maharaj's *guru-bhakti*, or devotion for Pramukh Swami Maharaj, was the driving force for the project now. The community could sense his deep desire to complete Akshardham as a tribute to Pramukh Swami Maharaj. For him, it was an offering at the feet of his guru. This led hundreds of sadhus and bhaktas to serve with tenacity and passion.

On 25 June 2017, Mahant Swami Maharaj met with sadhus from Robbinsville while he was in Atlanta, after having reflected on the many contributions of bhaktas in America and felt there was an opportunity to do more. "Akshardham is being built with the prayers and physical contributions of thousands in America. Even those from the wider Hindu community are making impressive contributions. I think it is important that we engage our bhaktas in physical seva too. I want you to organize a system whereby bhaktas from around the nation can come and serve for a few days at a time." The sadhus and leadership devised a system through which hundreds of volunteers started to serve for a few days at a time. This system would eventually play an instrumental role in the completion of the Akshardham Mahamandir.

In May of 2021, the community was startled by a sequence of events that made completion of the Akshardham Mahamandir seem near impossible. Mahant Swami Maharaj immediately refocused the leadership on BAPS' ethos of bhakti and seva. He publicly motivated bhaktas to serve in the building process to the best of their ability. The bhaktas answered that call to serve without condition.

Men and women from across North America committed to serving from anywhere between two weeks to two-and-a-half years at Akshardham to fulfill their guru's request. Most had never worked on a construction site, let alone on a traditional stone mandir project. And yet, all of them were willing to learn. Mahant Swami Maharaj recalled Pramukh Swami Maharaj's promise to the BAPS leadership in America as motivation and guidance. "Have faith in God and trust in the bhaktas. They will do whatever it takes to complete this mandir." Under the direction of the skilled artisan volunteers, these volunteers served and learned on "the job." The dedication and service of the 12,500 bhaktas were modeled after the countless examples set by their own gurus' bhakti and seva.

In July 2023, Mahant Swami Maharaj arrived in Robbinsville, New Jersey, to fulfill his seva and bhakti to his guru and the community. He kicked off the Festival of Inspirations, culminating with the public offering of Akshardham in the Fall of 2023. He celebrated the volunteers—the skilled artisans from India, the sadhus, and the men and women bhaktas from across the nation. **As a sign of his gratitude, the guru visited the mobile homes on campus where Indian skilled artisan volunteers, sadhus, and American volunteers lived together as a community.** A home visit by the guru, or a *padharamni*, in the Hindu tradition signifies the guru reaching out to bless a bhakta and his or her family. **Mahant Swami Maharaj also asked his attendants to sweep the dust from various points on the Mahamandir construction site. He placed the dust on his head as a sign of reverence for the bhaktas who served selflessly.** The guru was teaching humility and appreciation. He, too, was serving as the ideal sevak.

The guru knew that in building this Akshardham, the bhaktas were building a new version of themselves. Selfless seva and bhakti were means to excel on the spiritual path. **For Mahant Swami Maharaj, this spiritual growth, personal development, and social integration were the true success stories of Akshardham in Robbinsville.** Just as the building process had inspired this success, he was sure that this landmark of Hindu faith, culture, and architecture would build better people, families, and communities for as long as it stood.

THE AKSHARDHAM WITHIN

If bhakti is why Akshardham stands, if seva is how it is made, if the bhakta is who made it, if Bhagwan and community are for whom Akshardham is made, then **the guru is the one who inspires, creates, and sustains Akshardham—by his example of seva and bhakti.** Without the gurus' lives as ideals, Akshardham would surely not exist.

As bhaktas journey towards perfection and moksha, they feel the guru's humanly divine hand on their back. **They are never alone.** The story of the building and completion of Akshardham is just one example of that divine presence. Although they were not involved in the day-to-day construction and decision-making, Pramukh Swami Maharaj and Mahant Swami Maharaj led the community through their spiritual presence. From acquiring the land to completing the grand steeples with limited skilled help, it was an uphill battle for a community of Indian immigrants and first-generation Indian Americans who were balancing their professional and personal lives. The guru's humanly divine presence inspired them to keep going and giving, and to do so with a smile and without expectation.

The lessons from building Akshardham demonstrate how the guru wishes for bhaktas to live—in love, in selfless service, in harmony with all, and at ease. In Hinduism, the guru is the source of true knowledge—the knowledge of one's atman. **Akshardham stands as a testament to how the gurus have helped countless individuals discover their inner selves, the Akshardham within, while serving in Robbinsville.** This story of Akshardham beyond all else is a spiritual one composed to the melody of bhakti and seva. **If the stones at Akshardham could sing…these are the songs that would ring.**

Akshardham Mahamandir is one of the most nuanced and diverse visual representations of traditional Indian music, dance, religiosity, and social engagement. The 10,000 statuettes and the 12,500 volunteers bring people together through their song of seva and bhakti. It inspires others to listen, sing, and share.

7

Afterword: Your Song, Our Song

In his masterful short story "The Hungry Stones", Rabindranath Tagore (1861–1941) imagines the interactions between stone statuettes and visitors in a palace. Albeit conceived in a different context, the Nobel laureate's imagination fueled mine while on a midsummer late-night walk on the Akshardham campus. I wondered how different statuettes of deities, poets, celestial beings, and social reformers communicated with each other. What do they say to each other in our absence? What if these stones could really speak and sing? I would never know what it is they say to each other, but the stories shared in this book are my interpretation of what I heard ringing while amidst them. Now, it is time to sing yours.

Songs have an element of participation and animation that words in books do not. No song ever sounds the same twice over.

Although the stories from Akshardham are centered around the same core themes, there is variation in how they ring in people's ears and hearts. It is this variation that is essential in the experience of bhakti in Hinduism and at Akshardham. There is space for people to experience and articulate differently.

As a bhakta and musician, I also appreciate the limitations of words and ideas. There is only so much that can be said and written. Some things must be seen, heard, and experienced. They must be lived to be understood. One of my greatest regrets is that I was unable to experience the act of physically serving alongside the bhaktas during the last two years of the Akshardham Mahamandir building project in Robbinsville. Whatever the reason, it is a major blinder in my ability to thoroughly share the experiences of joy and development narrated by those who were fortunate to serve. This is why I insist that you, the reader, visit.

This collection of songs does not fully describe Akshardham as much as it tries to give context to what one witnesses and experiences on a visit. With the risk of offending the reader through repetition, I will repeat my greatest realization while writing. **People and their songs come first here.** This foundation was reinforced by Bhagwan Swaminarayan within the Hindu tradition and exemplified through the later gurus' lives in BAPS. **Bhakti and seva are the foundation of Swaminarayan Hinduism, with the bhakta as its voice, the guru as its inspirer, and the stones as its medium (and a beautiful one at that). The family built from the integration of various cultural communities becomes an example of what is possible if we** selflessly love and serve. Akshardham is the result—a haven for cultural transmission, inclusivity, spiritual solace, and social development.

Akshardham's completion is the first verse. This book is the second. And your visit, the third. The stones will sing for generations to all those willing to listen. In a few short years, their songs may become yours. Sharing is an important seva. Perhaps one day you will tell me, tell the world, what it is that *you* hear from the stones at Akshardham. Perhaps one day, as Ishwarcharandas Swami alludes to in the Foreword, *we* will sing *our* song together with the potential to "move millions" one step closer to an experience of spiritual growth—a mind and heart without corners.